LIGHTS
IN THE STORM

Thoughts And Lessons From Life's Stormy Path

Renee' Belle Isle Green

WESTBOW
PRESS®
A DIVISION OF THOMAS NELSON
& ZONDERVAN

WestBow Press books may be ordered through booksellers or by contacting:

WestBow Press
A Division of Thomas Nelson & Zondervan
1663 Liberty Drive
Bloomington, IN 47403
www.westbowpress.com
844-714-3454

ISBN: 978-1-6642-3587-8 (sc)
ISBN: 978-1-6642-3586-1 (hc)
ISBN: 978-1-6642-3585-4 (e)

Library of Congress Control Number: 2021910846

Print information available on the last page.

WestBow Press rev. date: 07/27/2021

CONTENTS

THOUGHTS AND INSPIRATIONS ALONG THE PATH 1

Lighthouse, Compass, Ships Wheel.. 3
Life Is A Rose Garden 9
Peace Like A River 13
No Rhyme, No Reason 16
Stuck In A Rut... 21
Bringing Up A Child A Proverb 23
Does The Donkey Need to Talk? 26
Sand Buckets... 29
Misery Loves Company!.. 34
Do Not Make The Pain The Issue 37
Life's Hard 40
Myths and Urban Legends.. 44
Peace In The Valley, Still 47
Don't Worry Be Happy 51
BEatitudes Attitudes To Be 54
Overwhelmed... 59
No Fault Insurance 62
Fresh Lemonade?... 66
What IF? 69
Pick Your Battles 72
Rooted 75
Shackled By A Heavy Burden... 78
Where's Your Baggage?... 80
No Time Like The Present 83
What Is Missing? 85

Sometimes You Have To Drink The Cup 88

Why Does God Whisper? 91

Peck-a-Little, Talk-a-Little.. 94

Nobody's Business... 96

HOT, HOT, Water 99

PRACTICAL LESSONS 101

The Ten Commandments..103

The Greatest of These Is Love..112

Who Is The Creator? 117

The Importance of You What Makes You Special............................. 119

The Potter 121

The Gold Miner 125

Build Your House.. 128

How Will You Grow? 132

HOLIDAY INSIGHTS...135

"A Little Dab A Do Ya!" 137

Empty Tomb EasterCookies... 140

Anchor, Mom... 143

Father's Day 146

Truth or Tradition? 149

References 155

THOUGHTS AND INSPIRATIONS ALONG THE PATH

Lighthouse, Compass, Ships Wheel

Psalm 46:1-3
God is our refuge and strength,
A very present help in trouble.
2 Therefore we will not fear, though the earth should change
And though the mountains slip into the heart of the sea;
3 Though its waters roar and foam,
Though the mountains quake at its swelling pride.

Today was a hard day. I needed someone to help me get through it all. It reminds me of so many times I needed to help my girls through their hard days. Sometimes it was so difficult. Everyone deals with pain some way, somehow. For me, this is one of those days, when you hurt so bad inside it must get out. So, I am letting it out.

As an adult I deal with my pain in several ways:

- **<u>Write</u>** – I write about it on my blog.
- **<u>Cook</u>** – yes even when it is 98 degrees. It is raining so I made homemade chili – good old good-for-the-soul comfort food, regardless the weather. Sometimes you just need comfort food for lunch, no waiting for dinner.
- **<u>Shop</u>** – OK it was only a run to the local WalMart for some essentials (unlike when my mom would go buy a hat or a new pair of shoes.)

One or all of those usually helps. Today I need all three. I will tell you that I did my devotionals first. Of course, it helped and led to my writing. However, when I am hurting, I must get busy. I am not a saint and reading scripture does not fix things immediately but it often helps me to think through what I have read while I am busy. Truthfully, if reading the Scriptures fixed everything immediately, I believe God would be finished with me here and I would already be in Heaven. As a Human I must deal with the world and all that happens. Devotionals are needed, but we all know it does not always fix things. We must apply the Word to the pain.

Maybe I do not deal with my pain on my own; maybe God uses others to help me deal. Or maybe it is just that when I am busy getting things done it helps heal the pain. I am sure some would say I am not dealing with what is hurting me. However, I was raised by a mom that taught, *don't sit sour and soak.* That is one of our Southernism sayings for, *toughen up, life is hard.*

While I agree to a point that moving on is the best thing to do, it is also important to walk through the pain. It also provides examples for others in your family to learn how to walk through pain. Children do not know how to deal with pain on their own. So, if you are helping your child through a painful situation, you need to teach them to talk through it with you. They watch you and you teach them through your actions.

What are they being taught? You are setting patterns for them as an adult. You need to teach them how to deal with pain in their life. It is not an automatic response and you do not want them growing up blaming God for bad things in their life.

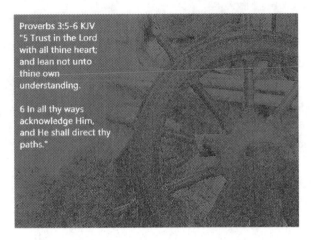

Proverbs 3:5-6 KJV
"5 Trust in the Lord with all thine heart; and lean not unto thine own understanding.

6 In all thy ways acknowledge Him, and He shall direct thy paths."

He steers us through rough waters.

What hurt today and why am I writing? Well, my cat has been ill and this morning he died. It was raining and my husband and I stood in the rain to bury him in the garden next to the Oleander bush.

We cried. Maybe you are saying, "wow, over a cat?" Well no, it was much more. It was just another domino in a long, long line of dominoes that included:

- My husband losing his job in a triple buy out three years ago and still not finding work.
- Being with my mom each day as she declined and died.
- My youngest daughter crawling out of a collapsed building in an E4 tornado that destroyed her college campus. She is safe by God's mercy but suffering.
- This all triggered my autoimmune battles.
- Planning a wedding out of state a week after, a graduation.
- Other family member's deaths.

We have been on a roller coaster ride that seemed to have no end. Maybe that was too much of a recital of our current life. Sorry. Just so you get the point, I am not a wimp, but sometimes there is that proverbial straw that broke the camel's back. It can be as little as waking up to find your comforting cat has died.

Now satan* attacks you during these times and he is not a respecter of age. He will attack anyone regardless of age, even your child early on as they go through tragedies in their life. You never know what the last straw will be. It may be something simple after many hard battles. Yes, the death of a pet may be the straw and it seems so tragic. I can remember everything from a butterfly funeral to a tropical fish funeral. I also remember my youngest losing her friend to cancer at age nine. I remember the pain and helping my girls deal with my brother's plane crash even as I was wheeling myself. They were ten and fourteen years old and very close to him, as was I. Even my husband was having a hard time with losing him.

I remember helping them through disappointments like not making the team or squad, missed opportunities, and first crushes. Pain comes in all shapes and sizes. Sometimes the little pains hurt more than the big ones. You must watch your love ones and not write them off with, *they will get over it*. Ignoring pain will just put it off until later and build a life time of not dealing with situations and a large collection of emotional baggage.

So how do you deal with pain? I love the symbolism of the nautical life. It is an easy way to show how God cares and directs during troubled times, the storms of life. If you are teaching a child about pain, a visual aide helps. Use a *lighthouse* that they can turn on in a dark room, a *compass* to use as you walk and talk, and a toy *boat* they can steer in the water. For yourself and others you are helping, you can just think through what the circumstances are and how God can guide through them using scriptures. Basically, all three of my symbols above point the same way, to Him.

- The lighthouse – my favorite – He is our lighthouse, a light unto my feet.
- The ship's wheel – Steering and guiding us through trouble waters.
- The compass – He directs our path through the narrow road

Psalm 139:3
"Thou compassest my path
and my lying down, and art
acquainted with all my ways."

He guides and directs our paths

> "When Jesus spoke again to the people, He said, "I am the light of the world. Whoever follows Me will never walk in darkness, but will have the light of life. *(John 8:12 NASB)*

> Thy word is a lamp unto my feet, and a light unto my path. *(Psalm 119:105 NASB)*

> Trust in the LORD with all thine heart; and lean not unto thine own understanding. In all thy ways acknowledge Him, and He shall direct thy paths. *(Proverbs 3-6 NASB)*

> Thou compassest my path and my lying down, and art acquainted with all my ways. *(Psalms 139:3 KJV)*

> This is what the *Lord* says— your Redeemer, the Holy One of Israel: "I am the *Lord* your God, who teaches you what is best for you, who directs you in the way you should go. *(Isaiah 48:17 KJV)*

Some may not understand how trials and rough times build character, especially small children. God gives discernment in these times if you ask Him for help.

> Consider it pure joy, my brothers, whenever you face trials of many kinds, because you know that the testing of your faith develops perseverance. Perseverance must finish its work so that you may be mature and complete, not lacking anything. *(James 1:2-4 KJV)*

God is always present for you. And, if you are helping someone else through a difficult and painful time, you need to continually reinforce that you are there for them as He is always there for them. Above all else, watch during hard times for open doors from the Lord to use that time to point towards Him.

*satan – he is a snake, so satan, devil, etc. are lower case in all of my writings because he is a lower case.

LIFE IS A ROSE GARDEN

T.V. has many shows telling you to come to Christ and your life will be a rose garden. Everything is all upbeat and happy. Then you have the flip side where people tell you that life is hard, even if you are a Christian, so deal with it. I think it is important that we have a realistic picture of our life in Christ. The truth is they are both right. Life in Christ *is* a rose garden but, you can count on it, life will be hard.

In the 1970's I was a member of the Atlanta Rose Society with my father. We even entered a few rose shows. I also tested for the Jackson Perkins Roses Company for a time. I learned so much about roses. Rose gardens are hard to maintain. There is so much to making the rose the beautiful flower it is before you cut it and put it on your table. There are four common problems in growing a rose bush.

2 Peter 3:14
"friends, since you are looking forward to this, make every effort to be found spotless, blameless and at peace with Him."

<u>Black spot</u> – a fungus that causes the leaves to drop and weakens the plant. The black spot in a Christian's life is sin and causes weakening in our daily walk; crippling us until we are of no use to Him. We are to be spotless.

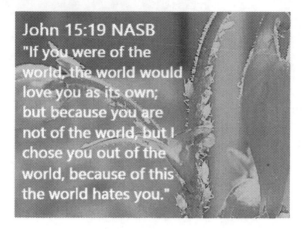

John 15:19 NASB
"If you were of the world, the world would love you as its own; but because you are not of the world, but I chose you out of the world, because of this the world hates you."

Aphids – suck the sap out and inject their saliva, which passes disease from one plant to another, weakening the plant and keeping it from proper photosynthesis. When we allow aphids in our life (parasitical non-Christian plans and lifestyles) to contaminate us with the ways of the world, we cannot grow in Him as He has planned. This is where we need to learn to be *in* the world and not *of* the world.

Where you are rooted will effect your spiritual life. Are your roots rotting?

Psalm 26:12 NASB
"My foot stands on level ground; In the congregations I will bless the LORD."

Root rot – roses do not like wet feet. They need proper drainage, so the soil mixture needs to be correct. The plant depends on its feet, or as we know them, roots. If they are wet all the time they will rot and the plant dies. As

Christians we too can get root rot. The soil we are planted in and the soil we plant our lives in must be properly conditioned by the Holy Spirit. If we are filling our soil with junk and rocks, then we will get root rot. This will cause us to be unfruitful, and we will wither up and die. What we read, watch, and hear (and what we allow our children to read, watch and hear) conditions our soil.

JOHN 15:2 NASB "Every branch in Me that does not bear fruit, He takes away; and every branch that bears fruit, He prunes it so that it may bear more fruit."

<u>Pruning</u> – you must cut a rose off the bush correctly if you want it to grow another flower. That means do not *hedge trim them across the top* and do not cut in the *wrong* place. It must be an angle cut above a five-leaf for another rose to produce. It is extremely specific, and it removes the bloom above the cut. The rose bush loses a bloom. If it is cut wrong it will not produce correctly, becoming ugly and without blooms. Then there is the winter pruning when the plant is cut to one third of its normal size leaving only the pencil width stems. It seems harsh and it looks harsh, but winter is coming, and it will brace the bush for the harsh times ahead. We must not shun the pruning of the Holy Spirit, especially when we are in a *winter* season. It will be specific and direct, and we need to trust those times when something specific is pruned from our life. Sometimes it will feel so harsh because winter has begun, again. Sometimes we think spring has come only to be hit with a harsh winter storm. If we allow the Lord to prune us correctly, we will produce fruit many times over regardless of the winters and their length.

God plants us as a rose in His garden. We will have black spot all around us to ward off. Aphids will constantly try to suck the very Christian life out of us and devour us. Root rot will try and sneak up on us and we must be constantly aware of where we plant our feet. Pruning is necessary and it will hurt but, we can trust the Master Gardner knows what is best for us. If we do not resist, we can grow from His careful shears and will produce even more beautiful fruit for The Gardener. And finally, we must walk with Him daily removing all the thorns of our lives that would hurt others and be a true beauty to the world of God's love for us.

> *...give thanks in all circumstances, for this is God's will for you in Christ Jesus. (1 Thessalonians 5:18 KJV)*

> *...always giving thanks to God the Father for everything, in the name of our Lord Jesus Christ. (Ephesians 5:20 KJV)*

PEACE LIKE A RIVER

Peace is sought everywhere. No matter the continent or country, people are looking for peace. Of course, there are those that destroy peace, but most want to find some sort of common ground and get along. According to the Merriam Webster dictionary:

> *peace* noun \'peso\ *(1) a state in which there is no war or fighting (2) an agreement to end a war (3) a period when there is no war or fighting*

The Baker's Evangelical Dictionary of Biblical Theology says:

> *The Meaning of Peace*. In English, the word "peace" conjures up a passive picture, one showing an absence of civil disturbance or hostilities, or a personality free from internal and external strife.

Isaiah 48:18,
"Oh, that you had heeded My commandments!
Then your peace would have been like a river,
And your righteousness like the waves of the sea."

Some want peace in their personal lives, between family members like siblings, parents, in-laws, even cousins. Others want peace at their school, or job. Maybe peace is needed in a church or neighborhood. No matter what kind of peace, it all starts with you.

1. First, and most importantly, you must have the Prince of Peace in your life, or all your efforts will be futile.
2. Secondly, you must daily seek peace. Sometimes it may even be a moment by moment, standing on His promises to get you through the situation.
3. Finally, you need to understand there is a reason we say, *Peace Like A River*. Not a lake, or the ocean but, a river.

That thought struck me this past week. I did a little research on what the Bible says.

> For thus says the *Lord*, "Behold, I extend peace to her like a river, And the glory of the nations like an overflowing stream; *(Isaiah 66:12a NASB)*

> If only you had paid attention to My commandments! Then your well-being would have been like a river, And your righteousness like the waves of the sea. (Isaiah 48:14 NASB)

A lake is a body of water, mostly still. The ocean goes in and out against the shore. But, a river, a river takes a journey. Life is a journey; peace is a journey.

Daily going forward, putting yesterday behind you. God's Word says it just, right. He will be with you on your journey, and His peace is there for you. There are many verses in the Bible about peace.

> Do not let your hearts be troubled. You believe in God; believe also in me. *(John 14:1 NASB)*

> Peace I leave with you; My peace I give to you; not as the world gives do, I give to you. Do not let your heart be troubled, nor let it be fearful. *(John 14:27 NASB)*

These scriptures should get you up shouting PTL and PTA. That is a Southernism for *Praise the Lord* and *Pass the Ammunition*. Because we know when you win one battle, another is just around the corner and you need to reload the ammunition. But we also know *He has already won the war* at Calvary!

I have told you these things, so that in me you may have peace. In this world you will have trouble. But take heart! I have overcome the world. *(John 16:33 NASB)*

On the evening of that first day of the week, when the disciples were together, with the doors locked for fear of the Jewish leaders, Jesus came and stood among them. *(John 20:19 NASB*

Again, Jesus said, "Peace be with you! As the Father has sent me, I am sending you. *(John 20:21 NASB)*

A week later His disciples were in the house again, and Thomas was with them. Though the doors were locked, Jesus came and stood among them and said, Peace be with you! *(John 20:26 NASB)*

And the peace of God, which transcends all understanding, will guard your hearts and your minds in Christ Jesus. *(Philippians 4:7 NASB)*

Let the peace of Christ rule in your hearts, since as members of one body you were called to peace. And be thankful. *(Colossians 3:15 NASB)*

May your life be peaceful like a river.

No Rhyme, No Reason

The headache wakes me every morning as it has since June 21, 2015. Some nights the nuero-pain blocker medication helps me sleep until 5AM. Some nights only to12:30AM or 3:30AM. No rhyme, no reason. I can take the minimum dose three times a day and be functional. It is what it is, and that is okay.

Looking back to Father's Day in 2015, I realize how far I have come. I can write, sometimes read several paragraphs, without starting over. No rhyme or reason to the damaged area's lasting effects on my brain's functions. So many tests, still no answers. On that day in 2015, it would seem there was not a rhyme or reason to what I was experiencing, or what was to come.

If I had been given a choice, I would have said, "No thanks Lord, just take me home." There would be many times I would ask Him for that in months to come. It was not a suicidal thought or depression issue, as doctors insisted, I would have. It was just I was in such pain, like I had never known. I knew pain and fear, I thought, until this happened.

June 21, 2015 - My head hurt for days. I felt, odd. Something was wrong. By Father's Day it was worse. Maybe the pressure, or maybe my brain bleed started small. Had it been a small bleed for days, then became the double bleed? No one knows. I remember going through the ER doors. My husband says I talked after the MRI. I do not remember that test. I remember fighting to not be put in the helicopter for the life-flight to Tampa General. Or, I remember my husband talking about it, I am not really sure. I remember the EMT guy's big handlebar mustache though. I think the bleeding increased in the helicopter ride. The brain can be weird in the details it retains.

I remembered the word *pray*. But I could not pray. I remembered, *need to pray*. I remember bits and pieces, phrases of Scripture. Not whole scriptures or references, just key words and phrases. God has a provision for anytime when we cannot pray. He thought of every detail.

> *In the same way the Spirit also helps our weakness; for we do not know how to pray as we should, but the Spirit Himself intercedes for us with groanings too deep for words; and He who searches the hearts knows what the mind of the Spirit is because He intercedes for the saints according to the will of God. And we know that causes all things to work together for good to those who love God, to those who are called according to His purpose.* (Romans 8:26-28 NASB*)*

The pressure of the air flight made head hurt worse. Maybe I bled more. When I arrived at Tampa General Hospital I had bled over and into the brain; a double bleed. It left a lesion the size of your little finger in the front lobe of my brain. Everywhere blood touches it kills brain cells, the only cell our body will not replace.

I was born with the DVA that had ruptured. All those years of migraines and tests never revealed the DVA. Why now? What rhyme or reason? Although I have little memory of the air flight I do know it was low, across the top of trees to keep pressure down. It was quick, or I was in and out and could not tell. I do not know. The gurney legs dropped down, and I briefly remember they rolled me across the tarmac and headed in to waiting staff. Then all went blank. My head hurt so bad.

I was scheduled for surgery. I must have come around, became lucid briefly. I remember a man standing there. In shorts and a ball cap, he looked familiar. He was traveling home from his Father's Day with his own father in another state when he got a phone call. He was one of our pastors, Dr. Dowdy. He arrived and was waiting when they brought me in off the tarmac. He asked to pray for me. Even though I know the Holy Spirit groaned, God knew I wanted to hear someone pray for me. God had sent someone to pray. The scripture I kept vaguely trying to utter I could not. Pray, it just kept coming back; one word. The Holy Spirit prayed for me and sent someone to pray for me out loud. Peace came over me. I hurt so much but, I was not afraid.

My journey started an hour earlier when my daughter in Montana called her dad to wish him happy Father's Day. Upon his description of my condition to her she urged him to get me to an ER. She thought I might be having a stroke. With God there are no coincidences. She got people praying.

She started with her long-time friend, Dr. Dowdy's daughter Liz. Liz got off the phone with her and called her dad. He headed to the hospital and was there before my husband coming from FL Hospital by car where he first took me. No rhyme nor reason, yet God's plan. The bleeding stopped; the pressure dropped. The surgery canceled. I am so glad they did not drill into my brain. Prayer changed things. It always does. Had I died their prayers would have still been answered. I would be healed and in Heaven. Sometimes we do not realize healing is here, or there. There was a rhyme and reason. I just could not see either.

I remember:

- ICU
- Plasma bags
- MRIs, EKGs, EEGs, CATs
- Angiograms
- Daily Dopplers
- My hands looked beaten; veins became unusable
- Funny compression bags on my legs.
- Room at 60°. The nurses in sweaters bringing heated blankets to Phil (yeah, some things you just stay mad about)
- Head surrounded by ice packs
- Headache, oh the headache
- Confusion
- Trying to talk

Would it never end? What was the rhyme or reason to all this confusion? Ten days in ICU then to the Neurology floor. The nurse did not like me praying.

After walking in and seeing someone praying with me his whole demeanor changed. Before that he had been fine. After that, not. He said doctor's orders were that I could go home once I was off my IV. So, he removed my IVs just hours after I had come to the floor from ICU. For some rhyme or reason, he had not liked what he saw. His demeanor changed. The praying had changed things.

After he pulled out my IVs I was discharged to home. I never went to a rehab. My IV arm began to swell. The seizures started. Back to the hospital I went for five more days. Rhyme? Reason? That nurse walked into my room; his face froze, and he left quickly. He never entered my room again. The admitting nurse had asked about my arm, so I told her. I guess he had been reported. Maybe God used me to have him looked into.

Only God knows His plans and reasons. He does not always tell us why. We can trust He has a reason and let it go. We do not need to understand our circumstances. Instead of why, ask God how He wants to use the circumstance to teach you. God is sovereign.

Since June 2015, I live with a headache, comfortably. Oxymoronic, I know. There are days it is totally intolerable, and I resort to packing my head in ice. Doctors still run tests, try different avenues of treatments. None have succeeded so far. There is no rhyme or reason why, in my way of thinking. I will never know all the *whys*. I just rest and know, God's plan, not mine. He has a rhyme and reason to the smallest details of our life. Again, God is sovereign. Some people meet me and think I am normal. Quit laughing. Some of you that know me are surely thinking, "She was never normal." There is a rhyme and reason for my pain. It is part of my life, part of my testimony.

> Rejoice always; *17* pray without ceasing; *18* in everything
> give thanks; for this is God's will for you in Christ Jesus.
> *(1 Thessalonians 5:16-18 NASB)*

Not *for* all things, *in* all things. That is a really big difference. God is sufficient. I do not thank God for the pain or the circumstances that brought me to this point. I thank Him for His plan, His rhyme and reason for the details. I thank Him that He is sovereign.

We have no idea what pain people live with in their lives: spiritually, physically, emotionally, or mentally. Much of which seems to not have rhyme or reason. I guess what I am trying to impart is to trust God with the details. We do not need to know the rhyme and reason. Trust His sovereignty. As my headache subsides to the status quo of the day, I can move on with the daily routines. I do not fret over that I still have my headache or let it hinder me. It is part of my life. I can trust God's plan and that He has a rhyme and reason. I can trust in His sovereignty.

Stuck In A Rut

People are funny, we get into such ruts; predictable in all we say and do. *Stuck in a rut* is an idiom that means a boring lifestyle that never changes. We are just creatures of habit; we fall in comfort zones and stay there. This is ever so true of our prayer life.

Do you know what certain people will say when called on to pray? You know some that will start the same way every time, using the same key phrases. Some even say the same phrase over and over throughout their prayer. They are creatures of habit, *stuck in a rut* and comfortable. If we talked to each other this way, we would soon find ourselves alone. Sometimes I think we must bore The Lord to tears.

Praying is talking to God in conversation. You can talk to Him anytime and about anything. I had a woman tell me her husband was so spiritual because he prayed three times a day. I told her as Christians we can pray unceasingly. In other words, we are open in communication 24/7, talking and listening, always an open line with our Lord. If Christians keep a right fellowship with their Heavenly Father through prayer and reading His Word they *can* pray unceasingly.

So how should we pray? The model prayer, or Disciples Prayer, in *Matthew 6:5-13* is a good way to learn how to Pray (talk) with The Lord. This passage of scripture is often called The Lord's Prayer but that is in John 17.

RENEE' BELLE ISLE GREEN

The model prayer: No Repetitions here.

1. Acknowledge Him
2. Praise Him
3. Thank Him
4. Seek forgiveness from Him
5. Intercede for others
6. Pray in Jesus' name.

The Lord gave us a particularly good model to learn to pray and it is sad so many simply use it as a recital piece only. Praying should be intentional, like you mean it, not a recitation, habit, or duty. It helps me to visualize as I pray. "Lord, I need the wisdom of Solomon, or the courage of Daniel." I have prayer lists, but I do not pray from top to bottom, or even all at one time. The Lord will bring them to mind throughout the day, often awakening me in the middle of the night and laying them on my heart. It took me a long time to learn not to simply *pray the list*. When you are in a fluid conversation with The Lord, the Holy Spirit will recall those on your list in need throughout the day.

Prayer is a gift from God, a blessing that, allows us to communicate freely. Sadly, we often abuse the privilege and misuse the gift.

Bringing Up A Child A Proverb

I once told a child of mine it was going to take Heaven for them to make eleven. They were ten years old and driving me insane. Good news. We both made it. She graduated College, and is married with kids. The point is not that we get pushed to our limits with our kids. It is what we do with that limit's line. It is just so easy to give into them.

Drawing lines, making boundaries, we make them, we move them. Why? When did we become so pliant as parents?

> Train up a child in the way he should go. Even when he is old, he will not depart from it. (Proverbs 22:6 NASB)

This scripture is a proverb and *not* a promise. They still have free will. At some point they become adults and will make their own choices. Choices have consequences. Choose the consequence by the choice you make. Bringing up a child and nurturing them in the Scriptures, God's Word, prepares them for making good choices. It helps them to decide to yield to the Lord and His hands. Will they yield to the master's plan, allowing Him, the Potter, to shape them?

The Potter molds the clay. The clay does not tell the clay what to do. Sometimes there is harsh molding, sometimes, gentle strokes, so light and fine, but there.

Raise her up to be the woman that when her feet hits the floor the devil says, "Oh NO! She's up!"

R8GREENDESIGNS.COM

It depends on the desired effect. Changing the design midstream does not add to the finished project. It weakens it and sometimes destroys it. Sometimes we are potters for others. Remember, just as God is the Potter to His children, you are a potter to yours. Parenting is being the potter. It is a long and tedious process. Taking your hands off and letting them spin out of control results in catastrophe. Sometimes they are shattered forever. Although, The Potter never makes mistakes, we do as clay molders. Will there be flaws and defects? Probably will. We have them and we have The Potter molding us. We are such stubborn clay.

Firm molding through hands-on or tough love seems harsh to the clay. Call it what you like, really loving them calls for tough times. I taught mine that every child has a right to a place to sleep, food to eat and an education. And I told them (many times to their chagrin) that nowhere does that mean they get their own private bedrooms with all the smart technology. Nowhere does that mean they get designer drinks at the local cafe, lobster, steaks, and expensive desserts. Nowhere does that mean they get private school when homeschooling or a local good public school is available. I raised mine with no technology in their bedrooms. Computer was in the family room. They had an alarm clock, and extension to our landline for group schoolwork or team calls. No cell phones, computers or music technology were in their room. They could take a player in to listen to music quietly as they studied. No head phones. That was a place to sleep and study. They were *class-A* personalities, in public schools, they each obtained Five Varsity letters. Education at church and school came first. They earned the plus treats. They were guaranteed a place to sleep, peanut butter sandwiches or school lunches, and bus rides to school. They earned their own bedroom, waffles, pancakes, packed lunches, home-cooked meals, fast food trips, and all the activity fees plus mom's taxi to all the extracurricular activities. I put as much as 30,000 miles a year on those taxi's and as many of their friends as that minivan could carry.

Yes, we gave up the upgrades to a bigger house (we had 1500 sq. ft), fantastic vacations, my career job and all that would have afforded. I worked at their schools instead. But, as they strove under my boundaries to achieve, we did all we could to enrich their lives. We still took beach trips occasionally, camped, hiked, and went to the water and amusement parks in summer. You just need to set boundaries by the best children's manual, The Bible, and stick to them.

If you are raising your children with champagne taste on a beer budget, as the colloquialism says, then it is time to take a step back. Why put the pressure on kids to live that way? Why put that kind of pressure on the family? Is it because of our desire to fit in for appearances sake? Designer labels on clothes are not wrong, unless they are sweat shop made or fund ungodly programs. I bought labels when they were on the sale rack. I never bought for the sake of the label. If it was the best buy, then that was fine. There was such satisfaction in getting something they wanted on sale. There are good clothes, foods, etc. that are not the best appeal to the world. Teach good stewardship. Why care what the world thinks? Why teach a child to follow the world's styles when it is not okay with God? What kind of stewardship are you teaching them? What kind of life will they try to lead on those kinds of values when they are on their own?

God's opinion matters, the world's does not. It may be painstaking to detoxify your kids and give them a reality check, and by that, I mean a God check. It may take a lesson on *The Beatitudes: Attitudes to Be*" (In Practical Lessons at end of book.) But it is much better than the judgement day check we will all receive, both parent and child, if we do not realign ourselves with Biblical values.

Does The Donkey Need to Talk?

Numbers 22:28
"Then the Lord opened the mouth of the donkey, and she said to Balaam,
"What have I done to you, that you have struck me these three times?"

My mother had a best friend for eighty-five years. Delores and mom were maid/matron of honor at each other's weddings. Delores' daughters and my siblings and I grew up like cousins and in fact attended each other's family events. We have a lot of memories. They came to mother's funeral and sat with family. One of my favorite memories is from my bridal shower that Delores hosted at her home. She invited about sixty women from our church. At that time, they had been best friends for over fifty years. Delores could not resist a good tongue in cheek joke on my mom. As an ice breaker every woman had a Bible character's name placed on their back as they came in the door. Once everyone was in the door we were instructed to go up to people and ask questions to try to figure out whose name was on our back. The women would look at the sticker on your back and answer *yes or no* to questions to help you figure out who you were.

Delores had put Balaam's uhm ... *donkey* on mom's back. Okay, think the *gasp* at the end of the horse race scene from *My Fair Lady*. It is still talked about 45 years later. It was straight out of the Bible she said.

God has a sense of humor too. In tough times, in our rebellious times, He gets our attention one way or another. Numbers **22** tells the story of Balaam, a greedy man who the King of Moab asked to curse the Israelites because they were afraid of them. On the trip to curse the Israelites God blocked the path of the donkey and when Balaam could not get the donkey to move he beat the donkey. Then God had the donkey speak to Balaam and opened his eyes to the angel that blocked the path.

God blocks our paths and sometimes we try to bulldozer our way through in our own strength. Do you have a toddler or a teenager that just will not listen? Then you know how God feels with you when you are not listening. Sometimes we forge ahead through all obstacles, standing on the belief that God is going to get us through. You are not on God's path if you make your own way and you beat the messenger. God's word says:

> Now if any of you lacks wisdom, he should ask God, who gives to all generously and without criticizing, and it will be given to him. But let him ask in faith without doubting. For the doubter is like the surging sea, driven and tossed by the wind. That person should not expect to receive anything from the Lord. *(James 1:5-7)*

When you are on God's path there will be obstacles, but He will make a clear path around those obstacles. Beating your way through is not His way.

> No temptation has overtaken you except *something* common to mankind; and God is faithful, so He will not allow you to be tempted beyond what you are able, but with the temptation will provide the way of escape also, so that you will be able to endure it. *(I Corinthians 10:13 NASB)*

Does God need to make the Donkey talk to you today?

SAND BUCKETS

Children are growing up so fast now. With the ever-increasing advancements of technology, they are exposed to facets of life that some of us did not even consider until we were teenagers.

When do you teach them about Jesus?

I picked up my cell phone one day and I noticed it was a call from my daughter half way around the world. However, instead of my daughter's voice it was my four-year old granddaughter calling me from Cyprus. My daughter had dialed my number and handed her the phone in exasperation. Over the past two weeks she has asked questions about Jesus and satan*. When she asked why God just did not kill satan, since he was so bad, it was time to let her ask grandmom the 1000 questions. After all it happened to a villain in one of her stories. He was killed for being so bad. My daughter tried to tell her that bad people did not love God and Jesus. Bad people choose to be like satan* and do bad things. So, when they die, they go to live with satan instead of God and Jesus. It had all started the morning before. Audrey informed her mom she was sending Santa an email to tell him not to give satan any presents because he was so awful. Then she started asking her 1000 questions. Kids say the most precocious things ... and ask them as well. She never got around to asking me the "why God did not just go ahead and kill satan*" question. However, for fifteen minutes she asked me all kinds of other questions about being good, being bad, God, and satan*. She then asked about where her Grandpa (my dad) was in Heaven and she wanted to know about hades (I do not use hell around her so she will not inadvertently blurt it out and people think she is learning to cuss.) Obviously, she is truly contemplating the difference between good and evil.

Through the years different people have voiced their opinion over teaching children about God too early. They infer that there is no way they can understand. But Jesus said:

> Let the little children come to me and do not hinder them, for to such belongs the kingdom of heaven. *(Matthew 19:14)*

> ...and how from childhood you have been acquainted with the sacred writings, which are able to make you wise for salvation through faith in Christ Jesus. *(2 Timothy 3:15)*

How early is too early? Teaching children about God and good behavior should start from their first breath. From the music they hear, to your blessings and prayers, these are absorbed just as much as those baby videos and nighttime musical sleep aids. You know the world is bombarding them every turn they make with worldliness from the moment they arrive here. Children are always learning and observing even if not grasping the concept. Exposure to good and God's ways prepares them for their ultimate decisions in accepting God or rejecting Him. God expects us as parents to protect them from the world and show them Him. So how do you decide when and how much information to give a child. I will try to give a brief synopsis. Think of it like this:

Take time to fill their 'buckets'

Proverbs 22:6
Train up a child in the way he should go: and when he is old, he will not

Imagine that your infant arrives on this earth with an empty sand bucket. It is every parent's job to raise that child with their buckets.

CONTROLLING: The parent will walk through life holding the child and the bucket deciding everything that goes in the bucket. That may work in the first few years, but what does the child learn other than being a puppet or robot – a *mini-me of* the parent. Their views of God will be shallow in that they never learned to seek Him and His truths; they just repeat what they are told.

INDULGING: The parent sits the child down on the ground and gives them the bucket loaded with all the information and toys of life. They want their child to have it all and everyone to brag on them. They want them to have all the advantages and everyone to pat them, the parent on the back for their smart, successful child. They overwhelm the child with knowledge and trinkets, taking away their natural pattern of mental, emotional, and spiritual growth. The children are *force fed* life way too fast. God is in the mix, but He is not clearly defined. He is on equal footing with appearance, education, and success.

SELF-CENTERED: The parent may seem to be over-indulgent. In truth, they find it easier to give things instead of time. So, while indulging the child in their whims to over flowing their buckets too fast, they are doing it as a baby-sitter device so that they, the parent, have more time for themselves. They may do the obligatory 'take them to Sunday School, life groups, church and/or VBS but, will do little to influence their child in spiritual matters themselves. These parents are self-centered and are obsessed with their own buckets to fill. If their child learns about God, it will be on their own as their parent has little interest in their spiritual life.

INVOLVED: The final parent type is the parent that is prayerfully seeking how to raise their child. They have the manual, God's word, before them. Their child comes here, and they hold them in one arm and their bucket in another. The time comes when they sit the child down and help the child to select things to put in their bucket. At times, the bucket becomes heavy, and they help their child carry the bucket. The time will come when they can carry two buckets. They hold on to their young firmly at first, and then as they grow the palm loosens ever so slightly and finally opened. The child is on on their own. However, the hand is always outstretched ready to grasp or be grasped throughout their life.

I wanted to be involved. I was sometimes criticized by other types of parents for being always present. My daughters wanted to be involved parents as well. The hard part is knowing when and how much to give their child for their bucket. Taking time to listen to your child and what they are asking is so important. That is how God treats us.

God draws us from the time we are born. Jesus said:

> No man can come to me, except the Father which hath sent me draw him: and I will raise him up at the last day. *(John 6:44)*

> And I, if I be lifted up from the earth, will draw all men unto me. *(John 12:32)*

As parents we are His tool. He uses us to guide and teach our children in the ways of the Lord. And He teaches us to recognize their need for God, and to respond to His call.

Listen to what your child is asking, and they will let you know what they are ready for in the way of information. My granddaughter wanted to understand right and wrong. So we answered her to the best of our ability. We will make errors but, we pray and ask for wisdom as we talk to them. Four is not too young for them to understand right and wrong and start to ask questions. When they understand they will quit asking that question.

Involving older siblings, parents, aunts, uncles and Sunday School teachers, even minister, is equally important. Sometimes we hear them ask over and over and sometimes they do not grasp our answer. Do not squelch their asking, find the answer.

Another important thing to remember is that no two children are alike. That in no way means one is less spiritual or not as smart. Allow each child to grow at their own pace. Treat each child as unique and peculiar unto the Lord. That is how He treats us.

satan —I refuse to give him any status of importance. He is a snake, so satan, devil, etc. are lower case, as he is one.

MISERY LOVES COMPANY!

You start the day and you wish you did not have to get out of bed. You know it is going to be more of the same. Every day is the same. 2020 virus quarantine will long be seared in your mind. The kids or spouse have gotten on your last nerve. Or, maybe the loneliness of solitude is overwhelming.

You miss the days you once dreaded and/or some of the problems have multiplied. Was it just a few months back?

- You had to go to school with, work with or see someone you knew would ruin your day all over again.
- You feared your job was going to be lost in the company's downsize.
- You did not have enough money to pay the bills.
- You had papers to write or a pile of unending work; impossible quotas to meet.
- You had a love one with terminal or chronic illness you could not see enough.
- Or, maybe you were the one that was sick and had so many appointments to schedule.
- You were losing your home or had already lost it.
- You hated your job, or you lost it.

So much misery you dwelled on, making you miserable to be around. Then suddenly the whole world imploded, turned inside out and upside down. Now you know real misery, right?

Remember the song you heard as a child, *everybody hates me, nobody loves me, guess I'll go eat worms?*" Misery *loves* company, well usually anyway. Sometimes you just want to be left alone. No one has been down the road you are going down. Woe is you. Self-pity parties are very common. They are the easy way out when you do not want to face your circumstances.

Are you laughing at yourself yet? You should be. Laughter is good. Sometimes we laugh just because we do not want to cry. Go ahead, wallow in your misery. Make everyone miserable with you. Whine on the phone, social media, in your emails to anyone that will listen. Life is just not fair to you. It is supposed to be fair because you deserve fair. Life should not be hard for you. You are a Christian after all. How Christ like is it to have to suffer?

I hope I made you think just now about how you are responding to whatever circumstances you are facing. During this time of the pandemic and all of the surrounding life issues, Christians are succumbing to the fear instead of walking through it with their Lord.

Do you know Who feels all these feelings before you do? The circumstances first go through His hands, Jesus' hands. Everything that hurts you, that touches you, He feels it first. Everything that happens to you *happens* to Christ first. Do you understand?

When something bad *happens*, right then and there He filters it through His nail pierced hands. We think of His suffering on the cross, dying for our sins way back then. We do not think of Him hurting now. When we are hurting, we forget He is hurting right along with us. Right now, in the here and now He hurts along-side us. Jesus wept when Lazarus died. He grieved with Martha and Mary. He feels with you as well. All your circumstances pass through His hands long before they touch you.

> For I know the plans I have for you, declares the LORD, plans for welfare and not for evil, to give you a future and a hope. *(Jeremiah 29:11 ESV)*

You are not alone, ever. He knows and He cares. Tell Him how you feel and feel His presence with you. You have a Savior that will always be there to carry your load. Concern over your circumstances is okay but worrying over them is not.

REMEMBER:

> No temptation has overtaken you that is not common to man. God is faithful, and He will not let you be tempted beyond your ability, but with the temptation He will also provide the way of escape, that you may be able to endure it.*(1 Corinthians 10:13 ESV)*

The Holy Spirit is the way of escape, the Power. This means that He will not allow you to go through more than will cause you to lose your faith. It does not mean He will not allow more than you can handle. He handles. He is right there to carry you through. Keep remembering, your circumstances were filtered through His fingers first. He felt them before you. Filtered, removing anything that would not be good for you.

> …in everything give thanks; for this is God's will for you in Christ Jesus. *(I Thessalonians 5:18 NASB)*

If His light is shining through you, you cannot be miserable. Smile and mean it.

Do Not Make The Pain The Issue

My mother would always steer clear of people who gave organ recitals, as she called them. They were downers, depressing people. It was always a mistake to ask them, "How are you?" They never got better, something was always wrong, yet they were at the mall, in church, at the school function. They sounded as though they were dying yet they looked and acted fine.

Many of us have our issues, our daily battles. I have to say my chronic condition is a struggle. Mom and dad raised us that if you were this side of the grass to get on with your life and bear up under whatever you are going through. Physically it is hard I know, trust me. I will not give you an *organ recital* now, so do not worry. In our family as a child, unless you had a fever or could not keep your food down, you went to school. Later on we got jobs and the rules were the same. As long as you lived under my dad's roof you went to work regardless. My father had a great work ethic as did most of his generation. He went back to work a month after he had his right lung removed and worked for eighteen more years. It is a mind-set, mind over matter. You do not mind, it does not matter.

Work ethic seems to be a vanishing concept. People would rather complain about what needs to be done or how hard it is to do what needs to be done. I had a young college man as an employee once that could not get done what I needed him to do because he said he had a papercut. He also would complain, "It's too heavy." Once he said he did not do ladders. So I climbed up to do what needed to be done and he realized he had allowed his boss, a senior climb a ladder in his stead. One occasion he complained to another supervisor his foot was hurting so he could not carry boxes. Then I came around the corner in my braces with a box in my hand. He was forty years younger. When his mother came in to offer an excuse one day for him not coming to work, I realized where his entire whiney attitude came from. From that day on we tried our best to make him into an independent young man and a reliable employee.

Down deep I think it is simply that many people need someone to look at them and give them validating attention. There is a legitimate time of sickness or injury but using it for attention or to make your life easier just makes you a hypochondriac.

Unfortunately, many people carry this mentality into their spiritual life as well. I call them spiritual hypochondriacs. It is no secret that in the Christian life we have ups and downs, mountains, and valleys. Some people hit the valley once and get stuck. They clamp down on the experience and never get better. They remember when things were better, when God blessed them, and everything was smooth. Every time you meet them, they have the same prayer request. Let me insert here I am not talking about a long-time illness, financial situation, loss loved one, etc. I am talking personal growth. Many times, we do go through an extended time in the valley because we do not grow in the Lord, we do not learn what He brought us there to learn. So there we stay as He teaches us the lesson over and over until we finally get what He wants us to learn. Our daily life is about growing more in the Lord. If we get stuck in the valley, we are not feeding our spiritual life. We are probably not reading His word, praying for others, and talking with Him daily. We need to fellowship with other Christians who help pull us along and we in turn pull them along when the road is hard. If we are not doing His work and helping others, then we are in the selfish *all about me mode*. It is the spiritual version of *look at me*. These kinds of people become cancers and spread through a body of believers, making them all a *doubting Thomas* and *woe is me* Christians. Nothing the devil likes better than to get Christians into spiritual hypochondria.

Got pain? Do not make it an issue. Take a time of rest if you need it, let it heal or get better, but do not wallow in your illness. Doctors say positive attitudes and a *can-do* spirit helps people heal faster. For Christians, the same attitudes apply. Sometimes the valley is long; it is the drudgery of day-to-day living, which, never-seems to end. But the Scriptures tell us,

> Consider it a great joy, my brothers, whenever you experience various trials, [3] knowing that the testing of your faith produces endurance. [4] But endurance must do its complete work, so that you may be mature and complete, lacking nothing. *(James 1:2-4 HCSB)*

Some coach has taken credit for the *No Pain, No Gain* concept even though it came from the Bible. Let people hear of your journey, counting it all joy, with expectation of what the Lord is going to accomplish in your journey.

Do not make the pain an issue.

LIFE'S HARD

These things I have spoken to you, so that in Me you may have peace. In the world you have tribulation but take courage; I have overcome the world. (John 16:33 NASB)

Social media is swamped with everything from pity and woe, to beware and be scared. It is not that I do not understand these emotions, these fears, I do. I have lost so much in life through the years. My list is long. Losing loved ones, friends, children you never hold, jobs, homes and so much more. Life is filled with hard loss and hurts.

I lost a sibling tragically. I did not understand and God was not asking for my understanding. I know death up close and personal. I have watched it suffocate. I watched my dad crash. I watched his lungs suctioned. I sat by mother's side the last three days of her life. God never asks me to understand or approve His plan. Through His Scripture He instructs me to trust and obey; to have faith.

I have walked through hard times of jobs lost, savings and retirement gone, car and home lost. No income is a very hard walk of trust. Not just hard but, devastating and terrifying to not know how you are going to buy food and pay bills. But God has a plan. I am never asked to like or understand the circumstances I pass through on this journey called life. He only asks that I just stand on His firm foundation and trust His plan. It does not matter if I ever understand the reason this side of Heaven. He only asks me to trust and have faith.

Many have lost faith and trust in God and are living in fear. They have lost how to stand on His foundation. They live in fear. The 2019-2020 pandemic has brought the world to a standstill. People are finding reflections of their inner-self revealed for all to see. People are scared of food shortages and supplies and of loss of jobs.

Seniors in High Schools are missing end of year events including graduation. It is hard, I know and I understand. My entire senior year was a nightmare. I witnessed a stabbing the first month of my senior year. Our entire world was shattered as we were stopped from having football games, extra-curricular events. I had to testify at a trial, I was threatened. I did not go to homecoming or prom. I had worked all summer with eight band girls teaching them to twirl a baton. I made them three uniforms each. That was twenty-seven uniforms that saw little use when my senior year world was turned upside down. A boy was stabbed in the heart in front of me. I was traumatized. Memories I want to forget. I was 16 years old. My twin brother was the drum major and he turned to protect me and push me out of the way of the five boys attacking. The deputies took four of us as witnesses. They allowed my brother to stay with me. It was an away game and cell phones were not invented. My parents met the busses and heard there was a stabbing. There was confusion and fear for a time as brother and I did not get off the bus. Someone finally told them that they thought we were ok, and I was a witness. My parents had to go home and wait for a call. They waited a couple of hours to hear we were okay.

The deputies caught all but one of the five that night. The guy that stabbed the boy in the heart got away. At the sheriff's office they lined up the ones they caught directly in front of us, eye to eye. No two-way mirrors; we were face to face accusing them less than three feet away. Early the following Monday morning I walked into home room. There at the back sat the guy I saw stabbed the boy in the heart the previous Friday night. I did not know his name. Our classes were large. My fear was real and unimaginable. I asked the teacher to be excused and went to the principal's office. The detective was in his office going over Friday night's events. He remembered me from the witnesses and I told him the guy they were looking for was upstairs in my homeroom. He went up and arrested the boy.

The threats came on the phone in the middle of the night. Dad took the phone off the hook. The threats and more came at school then. At sixteen, and the youngest of my parents' five children, I was strong, yet I was being eaten inside with anxiety and fear. The doctor finally gave me a mild tranquilizer to calm me during the turmoil.

Our school was suspended from all extracurricular even though the rest of the students had nothing to do with the five that committed the attack. It was corporal punishment, unjust and unfair. We were teenagers missing out on our senior year events. My 17th birthday came and went.

Two witnesses dropped out due to threats. I was having nightmares; I became afraid of the dark. The trial was horrible. The tranquilizers did not help. The stress and fear were overwhelming. I alienated friends, and eventually my high school sweetheart.

Our senior year seemed lost but, weeks later we got back our extracurricular activities after my dad and another father (dad was on the Georgia Bar and the other father a D.A.) threatened to shut down all sixty-four county high schools if the superintendent did not lift our school's extra-curricular ban. That got the school board's attention. You do not punish all the good kids for five kids doing bad things. Our teams, band, chorus, drama, etc., were able to do some events, finally. I graduated the following May at 17 years of age; it is a blur in my memory. All the years of dreams for my senior year were gone. I do understand what the seniors during the shutdown of the pandemic are going through. Part of graduation is a rite of passage into adulthood. It is a time of reality checks, character growing and balancing of reactions.

Life is hard and growing up means you need to realize bad things happen in life. Sometimes it causes inconveniences and many times heartbreaks, even tragic endings. My graduating year was just half way over and I had finished the trial and my school year. In the next six months I would take leaps in growing up fast and hard. My dad was diagnosed with lung cancer and had his right, three-lobe lung removed in the fall of that year. I was only seventeen years old and my world kept collapsing. I kept having problems with sleeping. I contracted pneumonia and had to withdraw my first semester of college. My dad was home and recuperating from surgery and I was recovering from pneumonia. It was a very hard year and a half.

High school senior year and/or college freshman year are not good for everyone they can be hard and traumatic. Whatever year of life you find hard, focus on the good circumstances and memories you do have and be thankful. Look for and acknowledge God's hand in every detail. Count your blessings. You do not like the circumstances but, God has a plan. It is a time to grow and look for His will. I did not at first. I dwelled on disappointments and of lost dreams. I was raised and grounded in faith from God's Word. His Word does not return void. I finally found I was still on His firm foundation. He carried me through. Others will look to see how you handle your circumstances if you are a Christian. You may never understand nor see the purpose this side of Heaven and you need to accept that is okay. Will you learn anything through your circumstances? Will you grow? Will others see your faith in your circumstances?

Myths and Urban Legends

When I worked as an Assistant Manager at a Christian Bookstore I heard so many interesting *truths* from shoppers. They came into the store wanting to find a plaque, a bookmark, or maybe even a book containing their *truths*. Sometimes I asked them to show me in the Bible what they are looking for so I would understand the truth they wanted in print. It was my way of showing them if it was not in the Bible then it was not a truth. I found that most of these shoppers did not know if their *truth* was really in the Bible or not. They were often dismayed to find it was just something they heard a preacher, teacher or parent say and not based on anything from the Bible. There was no *truth* in the saying.

A woman came in and wanted a plaque that said, "when God closes a door, He opens a window." She was shocked we did not carry the saying on anything. I showed her the scripture she was referring to. I felt compelled to tell her my opinion about God and His using only the front door. I believe if the front door is not open then He is saying wait. He does not want you to crawl out through a basement window or out onto the roof through the attic. God's direction is plain, through the front door. Wait on Him to open the front door. Maybe you did not recognize the front door at first. He will show you to it if you wait on Him. Some struggle with this concept and you can tell by their reactions to circumstances around their situation. It is surprising how many times we say we want to get to know Him better and want to know His will. Yet, somehow, we never look to the obvious source for that information, His Word. We look for basement doors, windows, attic, and fire escapes, never the front door. Is it because many times it is closed, and we are to wait on His direction and truth?

Another example is the story of Noah. You heard it repeated and even sang about Noah and the Ark. You probably had books on Noah as a child. Through the ages people have taken what God's word says about Noah and the animals in the ark and changed it to say only two of every animal entered the ark, two by two. Look at what God's word really says:

> 2 You shall take with you of every clean animal by sevens, a male and his female; and of the animals that are not clean two, a male and his female; 3 also of the birds of the sky, by sevens, male and female, to keep offspring alive on the face of all the earth. *(Genesis 7:2-3 NASB)*

That is fourteen of each animal that is clean, and two of every unclean. Interesting that through the years the focus on the unclean became the *truth* for all the animals.

Another repeated myth concerns the weather. Growing up I remember that when there was an abnormal and out of season storm someone would say it was getting close to the end times because that is when the seasons would swap. That myth came from Padre Pio, a Roman Catholic priest who was quoted as saying, "You will know when that time is approaching because the seasons will change so the only way you will know the seasons is by the leaves on the trees." The Bible says the exact opposite in God's promise to Noah. He promised He would never destroy the earth by a flood again. Once again, someone said it and that made it so; a legend or truth began. Genesis says something entirely different. We should always look to His Word.

> While the earth remains, seed-time and harvest, and cold and heat, and summer and winter, and day and night shall not cease. *(Genesis 8:22)*

An often repeated *truth* is, "cleanliness is next to Godliness." No, that is also not anywhere in God's Word. You will not find those words in the

Bible. You may have heard, "God helps those who help themselves?" That saying is also not in the Bible. Did you know there were thirteen, not twelve, tribes in the Bible? Twelve is often referred to because the Levites were not given land, but the tribes were made up of Jacob's eleven sons and Joseph's two. There were thirteen tribes.

How many of these *truths* do you believe?

- Mary rode to Bethlehem on a donkey or other animal? **Luke 2**
- Three Wise Men? **Matthew 2**
- What about the unicorns mentioned in the Bible? The actual Hebrew word referred to a two-horned animal, but King James' scribes interpreted one horn and put in unicorn (nine times in the Old Testament. Contrary to popular myth, they did not *miss the boat* (Ark.)
- The popular Mizpah jewelry symbolizes love and friendship. These items are bought and quoting: *Genesis 8:49. "The Lord watch between me and thee, when we are absent one from another."* It was a covenant between Jacob and Laban based on their past differences, a warning that God was keeping an eye on them. No connection with love and friendship.

Do you listen to what others say, preach, and teach, accepting those words as truths in God's Word? Look for what they say and see if it is actually in His Word. As a Christian you need to know what the Bible says. You then must teach and walk what it says; not just keep passing on misinformation. Make a point of knowing what you are talking about. Do not repeat what others say. If you teach, teach what the Bible says and be prepared to give the reasons for what you believe based on Scripture. Know what you believe and why you believe. Make sure God's Word really said it before you repeat what you hear.

PEACE IN THE VALLEY, STILL

PSALM 23:4 KJV "Yea, though I walk through the valley of the shadow of death, I will fear no evil: for thou art with me; thy rod and thy staff they comfort me."

Peace in all, through Him

In 1937 Thomas Dorsey wrote "Peace in The Valley" for Mahalia Jackson. The lyrics are hopeful, a final day of peace. It talks about peace in the valley in the future. I do not need to wait for Heaven for my peace. And my future in Heaven will not be a valley. Valleys are in the here and now. Yet, I can have *peace* in the *valley* now according to God's Word:

> Even though I walk through the valley of the shadow of death, I fear no evil, for You are with me; Your rod and Your staff, they comfort me. *(Psalm 23:4 NASB)*

It seems with every year I find myself saying on December 31st, "next year will be better." I look over what has been and think it cannot get worse, but, then it does. December 31, 2019 was no different. Four months in to 2020 and the world closed down. Who knew? God knew because He knew when, satan* would raise his ugly head and strike. Fear and doubt became the norm. For me, I remember where I have been, what I have been carried through. I knew I only had to trust and obey. It was not an easy learned lesson though.

In 1990 my parents both had open heart surgery and my oldest brother was in a horrible car wreck that ruined his life. My husband lost job and I was delivered an unfavorable medical diagnosis. I was in a car wreck and there were several other calamities.

The year I picked up my oldest brother on his birthday to take him to his oldest son's funeral was a roller coaster of ups and downs. My nephew died too young from a brain tumor. We had a wedding, a birth, another car wreck, a death. Four Friday's in a row were ups and downs, a roller coaster of emotions. In a short span Dad died after seven months in hospitals following a stroke during his five-bypass heart surgery. We lost my middle brother in a plane crash. Then my nephew died from his brain tumor. We lost three generations of men, dad, brother, nephew, all gone in a short span. A spirit of fear hovered. It is how satan* attacks.

Trouble always comes in series of events, clump together. Another corporate buyout resulted in another job lost. My youngest daughter was almost killed in a collapsed building at college during an E4 tornado. That same week my 2-year-old granddaughter needed her stomach pumped from a bottle of cough syrup. My mother had just gone to be with the Lord after eighteen months of care following a fall. By February 4, 2008 I had a funeral, a daughter buried in a building, a granddaughter half way around the world having her stomach pumped at twenty-three months of age. Fear and doubt always hovers, ready to take over if you allow.

Just when you think things are turning around another year will tumble down on you. Another job lost through yet another buyout caused the foreclosure and loss of my custom designed house, my masterpiece. Yet the hard times were not over. We moved into a rental the realtor said was secure. Four weeks in, owners were foreclosed and house scheduled for auction. By 2015 my body had enough.

We will never know the cause of the double bleed stroke that resulted in the air flight of myself from Florida hospital to TGH's NICU. The DVA in my brain was congenital and waited six decades to rupture. The struggle to relearn, to keep on fighting was not just another hurdle. The medicines and side effects overwhelmed me. The perpetual headache from the lesion wore me out. The difference in the way people treated me hurt. Handicapped is not disabled. Brain damaged is not brain dead.

Circumstances I choose not to focus on, though ever present. I can write, but it is extremely difficult to read. Trial after trial, life in a fallen world is hard. When trials keep coming, falling one behind another like dominoes, you ask yourself, "when will the feasting years come? In the Bible Joseph had bad years followed by good years. King Solomon had great years, so then why not me? That is not a question from God? Eternal blessings are what He wants us to look at and count, not earthly. I will not allow *satan** to fill me with theses lies. I do have so many blessings. At times I do not see them because I start looking at the current circumstances. So many times, I could look at my life and think poor me. But, all I need is to look around me or, across the world, and see just how good my life is here. My very worse is still blessed by comparison.

No matter what you are going through, God does not make mistakes. With the bad comes His presence. If you focus on the bad of the circumstance you stumble. When you look back and see all He has brought you through you know He can carry you through anything. Look at all He has done for you. Do not let people tell you He will not give you more than you can handle. That is not what 1 Corinthians 10:13 means. It means He will never allow more to touch you than will cause you to lose your faith and give up. You might feel like you are going to, but He will be there, and He will remind you who He is and what He has done. He will carry you through; He is your out and escape. We truthfully have no idea how much we can handle anyway. Just remember that all goes through His hands before it ever touches you.

So, I will not worry about if a circumstance is going to turn around and end up well. Neither will I *borrow trouble* as my mother liked to say. I will take each day as He gives it, thanking Him for all the blessings that *satan** tries to make me forget by enticing me to look at the circumstances in my life. Life will bring what He allows. Good or bad does not matter as I can rejoice in Him regardless.

I will focus on my blessings, name them one by one. I have seven Grandchildren, wonderful blessings. My two daughters are blessings. We celebrated 44 years of marriage in January, 2021. God has blessed us by giving us another home of our own. I have doctors that tend to my needs. So much of the world does not. I have enough food and clothes and can share. He is allowing me to publish my book. He has given me so many blessings.

Today the forecast says clear blue skies. I can see a variety of large wading birds and listen to the songbirds in the trees. The coffee smells wonderful. My cat is purring. Bacon is sizzling. It is another day. God's creation is beautiful, He cares about every detail. He cares about me and all my details. He is not ignoring them; He is allowing them. I can take comfort in knowing they will work to my good and His glory as scripture says; regardless of whether they or good circumstances or bad. Blessings are everywhere.

> And we know that God causes all things to work together
> for good to those who love God, to those who are called
> according to His purpose. *(Romans 8:28 NASB)*

I am not able to do these things on my own. God left us a comforter, the Holy Spirit, which is in us constantly holding us up if we allow. I only need to talk to the Lord and say, "I am looking forward to today Lord. Help me to trust You today, keeping my focus on You and not whatever the day brings. Teach me."

*satan is always lower case in my writings because he is one.

DON'T WORRY BE HAPPY

A friend was talking with me this week lamenting my current troubles. Sounds like a Job's friend. She said she did not know how I stood it. I sigh. I know I do not, at least not on my own. Sometimes it is overwhelming and I get defeated and I cry. And sometimes I am just numb. It is not wrong that I have emotions. God gave me emotions. It is wrong when I give into them and let them control my life and outlook.

Others, especially kids, are always watching how we respond. Like it or not, we are examples God uses to help others prepare for something in their life. Sometimes what we go through helps others with what they go through in life, especially our own kids. The un-saved are watching as well. We are a walking testimony to our Lord Jesus Christ. If people know you are a Christian, can they tell it by your actions when things are not going smoothly?

The world says, *don't worry, be happy*. But they mean go party, go get drunk, do drugs, forget, and pretend it is not there in hopes it will go away. What do others see you do in a crisis? Every year on July 8th I think back when I drove my oldest brother to his oldest son's funeral who had died from a brain tumor on my brother's birthday. On the 25th of July I always remember my middle brother was killed in a plane crash. On June 2nd I remember dad's death after heart surgery. Dad and mom both had open heart surgery four weeks apart. Dad had a stroke on the operating table and was in the hospital seven months. My girls were four and nine years old and went with me every day to the hospital. This was the same time my oldest brother was in the wreck that kept him in the hospital for five months and left him disabled for life.

RENEE' BELLE ISLE GREEN

In 2006 mom fell while visiting at my sister's house in Kentucky. After surgery I brought her here to FL. My mom spent 18 months in rehab and died the last of January of 2008. I went almost every day as did my girls and even my granddaughter when they were in town. The week after my mom's funeral in Atlanta and the night before her memorial service here in FL, my youngest daughter crawled out of a collapsed building during an EF4 tornado February 5, 2008. It seems like every month there has been some trial, sometimes devastating.

I realized that since we married in 1977, over the years we have had some extremely hard times, including my husband losing his job three times in company buyouts. There were times in my daughters' lives that I was in bed with complications from lupus. My girls had to go through so much family pain growing up. So, what did they see?

This is not a pity-me list, this is a Yes, Jesus carried me list. Many reading have lists that contain much more difficult times. Make a list in your mind or write them down. How did you get through the hard times, on your own or with God? We tend to unconsciously pass on what has been passed on to us. Sometimes that is a good thing, and sometimes we need to break the cycle.

I cannot take credit; I am passing on what was passed *on* to me. What did my parents do when faced with circumstances beyond their control? Growing up I remember dad having ten or twelve deaths in his family over a two-year span. I thought funerals were the norm. I remember dad walking away from his huge corporate job over principles and them wondering how they would pay the bills. I remember when dad was diagnosed with lung cancer and his surgery. I remember mom having surgery when I was twelve and so many other hard times. Hard times are a part of life. What I remember most is my parents praying. Yes, I remember tears. I remember sometimes there was frustration and anger, briefly. What I remember most is that everything always came down to resting on their faith and trusting their Lord, reading His scriptures.

Come to me, all you who are weary and burdened, and I will give you rest. *(Matthew 11:28)*

Therefore, I tell you, do not worry about your life, what you will eat or drink; or about your body, what you will wear. Is not life more important than food, and the body more important than clothes? [26]Look at the birds of the air; they do not sow or reap or store away in barns, and yet your heavenly Father feeds them. Are you not much more valuable than they? [27]Who of you by worrying can add a single hour to his life? [28]"And why do you worry about clothes? See how the lilies of the field grow. They do not labor or spin. [29]Yet I tell you that not even Solomon in all his splendor was dressed like one of these. [30]If that is how God clothes the grass of the field, which is here today, and tomorrow is thrown into the fire, will he not much more clothe you, O you of little faith? [31]So do not worry, saying, 'What shall we eat?' or 'What shall we drink?' or 'What shall we wear?' [32]For the pagans run after all these things, and your heavenly Father knows that you need them. [33]But seek first his kingdom and his righteousness, and all these things will be given to you as well. [34]Therefore do not worry about tomorrow, for tomorrow will worry about itself. Each day has enough trouble of its own. *(Matthew 6:25-34)*

Searching His word for answers and guidance and prayer will always be the answer to all of life's problems. I can say that with conviction from experience. Otherwise I would have lost my mind. The one thing I remember about mom was her saying, "I'll pray about it." My mom was always teased about having camel's knees because she was on her knees praying at least once every day until she broke her hip in 2006 at 85 years of age. And even then, she was on her *spiritual* knees until the last year of her life when she had dementia. Life is hard. Do not shield your child or others from that fact. You are not doing them a favor. As you go through your trials they are watching. What do they see?

BEATITUDES
ATTITUDES TO BE

When I was in college in Atlanta, we traveled over thirty miles on Tuesday nights to a Bible study that sometimes had over 400 in attendance. A three-piece band a speaker; music and truths from God's Word were there each week. The concept was, *if you teach them they will come* and they did. We studied the Bible a passage at a time. I remember it was the first time I heard the phrase *The Beatitudes are Attitudes to be*. Most of what God wants to teach us is simple truths. We just like to complicate them.

In working in church activities with various ages young and old, you will know *attitude*. We probably get several doses a day of others' attitudes. God wants to teach us attitudes; *attitudes-to-be*. Jesus gave a wonderful lesson that we should learn, teach and pass on to others.

Remember your English lessons:

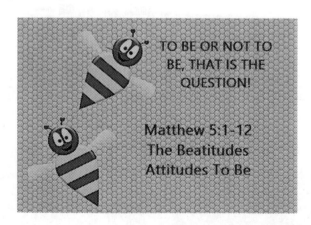

BEatitudes!

My paraphrase of **TO BE**: a verb and auxiliary verb present singular 1st person: am (I am)

- 2nd person: are (you are)
- 3rd person: is (he/she is)

Attitudes are something you *are* and by *choice*. A child needs to learn they *are* choosing their attitudes and those decide how they act. Actions have consequences. At the first sign of an inappropriate attitude I looked in my child's eyes and said,

> "You need to make a decision. Make a good one. If you continue in this _____ (name the action or attitude) then *you are deciding* and *choosing* this consequence (name it.)"

I wanted to teach them as early as two that they are *asking* for consequences by their choices. Yes, a two year old can understand the basic concept. If they are acting out, they choose to be punished. I learned not to let them blame me when they were punished. I wanted to encourage them to choose wisely and receive good consequences.

When I hear moms say, "he/she is in their terrible two years" or, "oh, he/she is carrying the terrible twos into the terrifying threes" I cringe. I really want to speak up and say, "Do not *claim* it, *change* it. Do something about it." Children should not control parents or home.

Parenting is a *small* minuscule picture on earth of our Heavenly Father's relationship with us. Remember what happens when you try to control your life; you are trying to control God? Makes a mess of things does it not? Same results happen when children try to control parents and homes. I see toddlers in control of large adults four times their size and I shake my head and think, "when did you hand them the keys?" I believe you can turnover control before they age two.

I will not mention which daughter, but one of mine wanted something in the checkout line and I said, "no". To which I received a tantrum, her first. I looked at her and told her she was embarrassing herself and me and that was no way to behave in a store. I told her to decide or I would have to embarrass her. She continued to scream. So, I dropped to the floor and threw a tantrum. She was mortified. She told me I was *m'bear-in-sing* her. I told her I would stop if she did. It worked. We were in Winn Dixie and a mom looked at me and said, "Oh, if I only had the courage to do that."

There were no more tantrums in the store. There are those that say not to humiliate your child in public. That is nonsense. Much of what is wrong with children is we are protecting them from good child rearing techniques for fear of what others will say or think. Or worse, what some ungodly professional in the world says will hurt the child's esteem. The world is not in charge of raising your child. You only answer only to God for how you raise your child. Any child still living at home and you are paying their bills, is your responsibility, your stewardship under God's eyes. I am sorry to say that an out of control teenager did not wake up that way one morning. It started years before when someone stopped parenting and handed over the keys. It is extremely hard but, not impossible to get those keys back and start over. God expects you do to just be the parent. With a preteen or teen, you start with a heart to heart of how it should have been and how it will be going forward. It will be hard as you take back charge. Keep reminding them their choices decide the consequences. Use God's Word.

God gave us a manual: BeAtitude (recognizing we *owe* all to God.) God is teaching that we are blessed and stewards of all that we have; we should be humbled and thankful not proud and greedy.

- 4"Blessed are those who mourn, for they will be comforted" (our BEatitude of *sorrow* for sin that brings repentance, recognizing when we do wrong and *really* being sorry.) God is teaching us we need to be sorrowful over sin and wrong doing; that we are dependent on the Holy Spirit to walk daily in Him and that we cannot do so without Him. Yield to the tugging of the Holy Spirit.

We know when we are doing wrong and ignore the tugging on our conscience. Ignoring the Holy Spirit within grieves Him, and we harden.

- 5"Blessed are the meek, for they will inherit the earth" (our BEatitude of *submission* to God.) God is teaching us to be quiet and rest in Him; not getting upset when we are wronged but to turn the other cheek and show His love to others as He has shown it to us. We are to be patient with others as God is with us.

- 6"Blessed are those who hunger and thirst for righteousness, for they will be filled" (our BEatitude is one of *sensing* our need for God and striving to be more like Him.) God is teaching us through the two things the human body can understand, hunger and thirst. These *needs* keep us alive and our hunger and thirst for righteousness are vital to our spiritual life just as food and water are to our physical body. Priorities must be set and followed. Putting God first makes everything else fall in line.

- 7"Blessed are the merciful, for they will be shown mercy" (our BEatitude is one of *showing* Christ in our actions.) God is teaching us that when we hunger and thirst after Him, our actions will show Him not us. This is our testimony in action. We show love for others as He has loved us. We give forgiveness as we are forgiven. We show compassion, pity, patience, just as we have been shown them by Christ.

- 8"Blessed are the pure in heart, for they will see God." (our BEatitude is one of seeking His Holiness.) God is teaching us to put away the world and seek only that which is pure. God cannot look on iniquity so having it in our heart separates us from Him. To see God, we must have a pure heart. Pure hearts come from what we put in our minds through our eyes and ears.

- 9"Blessed are the peacemakers, for they will be called sons of God. (our BEatitude is one of *solving* not creating problems.) God is teaching us to strive to get along and find good in others and situations; to establish peace through Him. Our light is to shine in a dark world bringing comfort and peace. As the saying goes, "if you are not part of the solution, you are part of the problem."

When actions display God in us and not us in the world, then we are part of the solution.

- 10"Blessed are those who are persecuted because of righteousness, for theirs is the kingdom of heaven." (our BEatitude is one of *selflessness*.) God is teaching us that when we take on all of these BEatitudes, the world will not understand. Sometimes you will be walked over, made fun of and some will even give their lives when following the BeAtitudes. This is hard for us as adults and certainly not something little children can grasp. We simple must teach them that sometimes, even though we are doing right, bad things are going to happen; people are going to hurt us. This is when it is even more important *to be* the BEatitudes through His strength in us.

- 11"Blessed are you when people insult you, persecute you and falsely say all kinds of evil against you because of me." (our BEatitude is one of *steadfastness,* standing strong in the power of the Lord Jesus Christ.) In America today, Christians are being picked apart and ridiculed. Christians will face more and more verbal, if not physical, persecution for standing on their testimony of Christ in them. During these times, our resolve may weaken, or we may become apathetic if we do not stand in His Power. There are times when I just get quiet and pray, "Lord, by the Power of the Blood, for the victory that *was won*, I bind this situation in the name of Jesus. What is bound on earth is bound in Heaven. I claim the *victory* in Your name." And then I move in His Power, not my own.

Learn the BEatitudes and pass them on. What is your BEatitude today?

OVERWHELMED

He is carrying me! He is not just fixing me, repairing me and patching me up, He is making me new!

Patched up or new?
Made over or patched?
New creature or covered up?
2 CORINTHIANS 5:17

Ever feel overwhelmed? I have so many times; actually way too many times. As a newlywed, on a new job and as a new mom when my children were young, there were many times when I just did not know how I could continue through another day. The worse years started in 1990 when my oldest brother was in his car wreck that ruined his life forever. Then both my parents had open heart surgery and dad had a stroke on the operating table. I also had to deal with my own abnormal tests result. My girls were four and eight years old, they still needed a mom. I was so overwhelmed. I just wanted that year to end.

The following year, 1991, was worse. Dad died and I was diagnosed with Lupus which resulted in my being in bed more than out some weeks. Right behind all this my husband lost his job and then my middle brother was killed in a plane crash. It seemed like unending years. During that time, my children would become overwhelmed as well with the issues our family were facing, problems at school, and troubles with friends. Children often act out during stressful family times. We do not think of their problems as huge because we can see the big picture, and many times the outcome down the road, if they would only be patient and learn from their trials. The big picture again; we are to our children, as God is to us. He sees and knows if we would only be patient and willing to learn.

We had many seasons of trials. We never did just one tragedy at a time; we always have them grouped together. It is a shame that God must re-teach us lessons. Once again, this week I have been overwhelmed. My husband was unemployed for over three years, during which time my mother died, my youngest daughter was in an E4 tornado and crawled out of a crumbled building. Later the same year on her campus an accident left her elbow in three pieces. During the same year, the bank started foreclosure on our home. I started a new forty hour a week job which included nights and Saturdays which left me exhausted. There were some other issues as well. I let the devil start whispering in my ear that all was lost and hopeless; that I was not up to the task God had set before me and that I was pretty much a useless piece of clay. No, I was not suicidal but, I was defeated. The devil loves to have us defeated. But I have friends and loved ones always praying for me and I was praying in earnest for mercy as well. And then He sent friends to me to talk to me, stand beside me and pray, lifting me up.

As God often does, during my *defeated state of mind,* He sent someone for me to help. I had a young girl crumbling before me that was overwhelmed. Like my children, I could see her problems were overwhelming her, but they would not destroy her. God knew I would go into *mom mode.* I had to turn her to the Scriptures I knew so well and tell her to stand on His promises.

> I will lead the blind by ways they have not known, along unfamiliar paths I will guide them; I will turn the darkness into light before them and make the rough places smooth. These are the things I will do; I will not forsake them. *(Isaiah 42:16)*

> No temptation has seized you except what is common to man. And God is faithful; he will not let you be tempted beyond what you can bear. But when you are tempted, he will also provide a way out so that you can stand up under it. *(1 Corinthians 10:13)*

As I shared these and other scriptures with her, she cried. I told her nothing is going to enter our life that is going to take away our Faith. God will provide a way out. Our part is to be faithful, not to solve. Our part is to trust and obey and lean on the everlasting arms. Our burdens are His to carry. Let Him. I was preaching to myself. God's timing, God's plan, God's will be done. *Keep me leaning on His Everlasting Arms!*

No Fault Insurance

In the early 1970's comedian Flip Wilson's introduced his famous skit, *The devil made me do it!* It was funny but, in a sad way, so true. When we are doing something wrong, we blame the devil*. It is human nature to blame *the other guy*. Kids blame the other guy all the time. They see their parents and other adults to it all the time. Sometimes they learn it at school, off the TV or from the videos. But it boils down to they learn it from their parents. Even if you do not do it, if you do not stop them from doing something wrong, then you have taught them wrong.

It is sad that so many are living in sin when we have the manual on how not to sin in hundreds of languages all over the world. The Bible tells us who sins, what is sin and what the consequences of sin are. Blame it on your upbringing? Blame it on genetics Blame it on the devil?

Here is how I explain sin. My family has a history of alcoholism in previous generations. My father, the youngest of eight children, watched all his elder siblings drink themselves to death, literally. Between the ages of 10-12 years of age, I attended so many funerals of my father's siblings and offspring, all related to alcohol. My father never drank. It was obvious there was a genetic tendency to alcoholism. My dad *chose not* to give into tendency and he never allowed alcohol in our home. He raised us all knowing we had that tendency as a possibility. My oldest brother *chose* to ignore dad's teachings and ruined his life, and his family's, with alcohol. When we *choose* to disobey, we *choose* to sin; we *choose* the consequences. Sadly, we inflict those consequences on all those around us. This includes family and even innocent bystanders; drunk drivers ruin innocent lives daily and walk away unscathed.

So, who is to blame? Can you blame God? Can you blame genetics, a bad home live; because you are poor, or the environment in which you live? Ultimately, the only one to blame is you. It was your *choice*. Why would anyone *choose* to be a drunk, ruin their life, be mocked, hated, and shunned? Bottom line because they *choose* to, no one makes them, they *choose* their life.

I *chose* never to taste alcohol, never to allow it in my life. It was my *choice*. I am not perfect. I have other sins I must *choose* not to do. I have an all-powerful God to strengthen me and help me with my *choices*. I cannot do it in own strength. I *choose* to sin; only I can *choose* to stop sinning. One step leads to the next but, the first step is always your *choice*, make it. Once you make that first step, get help if you need it. Sometimes people need help and there are wonderful organizations, support groups, doctors, etc. out there to help. But it takes your *choice* to take the first step to stop sinning.

WHO SINS?

> for all have sinned and fall short of the glory of God...
> *(Romans 3:23 NASB)*

> *"If we say that we have no sin, we deceive ourselves, and the truth is not in us. (1 John 1:8 KJV)*

WHAT IS SIN?

> Or do you not know that the unrighteous will not inherit the kingdom of God? Do not be deceived: neither the sexually immoral, nor idolaters, nor adulterers, nor men who practice homosexuality, [10] nor thieves, nor the greedy, nor drunkards, nor revilers, nor swindlers will inherit the kingdom of God. [11] And such were some of you. But you were washed, you were sanctified, you were justified in the name of the Lord Jesus Christ and by the Spirit of our God. *(1 Corinthians 6:9-11 ESV)*

[8] Now we know that the law is good, if one uses it lawfully, [9] understanding this, that the law is not laid down for the just but for the lawless and disobedient, for the ungodly and sinners, for the unholy and profane, for those who strike their fathers and mothers, for murderers, [10] the sexually immoral, men who practice homosexuality, enslavers, liars perjurers, and whatever else is contrary to sound doctrine, [11] in accordance with the gospel of the glory of the blessed God with which I have been entrusted. [12] I thank Him who has given me strength, Christ Jesus our Lord, because He judged me faithful, appointing me to His service, [13] though formerly I was a blasphemer, persecutor, and insolent opponent. But I received mercy because I had acted ignorantly in unbelief, [14] and the grace of our Lord overflowed for me with the faith and love that are in Christ Jesus. [15] The saying is trustworthy and deserving of full acceptance, that Christ Jesus came into the world to save sinners, of whom I am the foremost. [16] But I received mercy for this reason, that in me, as the foremost, Jesus Christ might display His perfect patience as an example to those who were to believe in Him for eternal life. *(1Timothy 1:8-16 ESV)*

WHY IS IT SIN?

Indeed, the Lord's hand is not too short to save, and His ear is not too deaf to hear. [2] But your iniquities have built barriers between you and your God, and your sins have made Him hide His face from you so that He does not listen. *(Isaiah 59:1-2 HCSB)*

HOW CAN WE BE SAVED FROM SIN?

...and He Himself bore our sins in His body on the cross, so that we might die to sin and live to righteousness; for by His wounds you were healed. (Isaiah 59:1-2 HCSB)

If you confess with your mouth, "Jesus is Lord," and believe in your heart that God raised Him from the dead, you will be saved. *(Isaiah 59:1-2 HCSB*

The Lord does not delay His promise, as some understand delay, but is patient with you, not wanting any to perish but all to come to repentance.*(2 Peter 3:9 HCSB)*

For God so loved the world, that He gave His only begotten Son, that whosoever believeth in Him should not perish, but have everlasting life. [17] For God sent not His Son into the world to condemn the world; but that the world through Him might be saved. *(John 3:16-17 KJV)*

All sin separates us from God. There are no worse sins. My sin makes me as big a sinner as the next person; although some sins have more consequences here on earth. If you sin, you *chose* to sin; you *choose* to be separated from God. You, and you alone, *choose* your consequences here on earth, and ultimately in eternity. Do not blame the other guys, your upbringing, or anything else. You have a *choice.*

*devil, satan – I know people capitalize the "S" or "D" but, I do not. I refuse to give him any status of importance. He is a snake, so satan, devil, etc. are lower case, as he is one.

Fresh Lemonade?

When you are squeezed, what comes out?

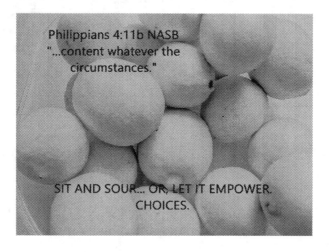

Philippians 4:11b NASB
"...content whatever the circumstances."

SIT AND SOUR... OR, LET IT EMPOWER.
CHOICES.

There is More to Lemonade Than Just Lemons.

Pressure, it comes from all sides. Home, work, friends, family, pressure, it is so stressful. Good things happen and bad things happen. Sometimes the bad outweighs the good. Why do some people have it easy while others seem to never catch a break? Every time you pick up a paper, turn on your computer or answer the phone you seem to hear nothing but heartache. After a while you could really get depressed.

The bumper sticker on the car in front of you reads, "Life, it happens." Someone you love is going to suffer an unjust circumstance. Something is going to happen that is just not fair. It happens to your children, your husband, your best friend, and yes, you. It may be something small, but like a splinter in a finger it hurts. It could be something huge that threatens to take you under. Pressure, it comes from all sides. Why?

The pressure is from a fallen world in sin. People get angry over the consequences of sin, especially when they suffer because someone else sinned. Who is to blame? *People sin because they are sinners; they are not sinners because of sin.* People choose to sin. Bad choices have consequences; *sin* has consequences. We all make bad choices; we all choose to sin. We are all sinners.

No one is righteous — not even one. *(Romans 3:10 NLT)*

Squeeze a sinner and you will get sin, every time. So, what do you do?

- Cry
- Hide
- Throw in the towel
- Run away
- Give up
- All the above

Yes, it is a cliché, "Life hands you lemons, make lemonade" or, "squeeze some carbon, get a diamond." I get tired of hearing that quote as well. Today you, or someone you know, will be pressured by life. The first impulse, because you are a sinner and sinners' sin will be what???? You are on the spot and must decide not to sin and/or help someone else not to sin. Worry is a sin. Blaming God is a sin. He did not create sin or sin's consequences, but for the time being He is allowing the devil to run the world because man *chose* sin. Christ died for those sins and that sinful nature. Claim that victory and do not believe the devil's lies. Just remember, God is in control, He is still on the throne, He loves you and He cares for you. *Trust* Him. Turn it over to Him.

- *Pray* first
- *Read* His word
- *Act* on His leading

- *Fellowship*/talk with other Christians
- *Encourage* other Christians

Ask God for wisdom today and *trust* Him for the rest. Ask Him to help you *trust* so you will grow your *faith*. A living faith accomplishes in our life what God wants us to have. A living faith walks on water.

> [22] Immediately He made the disciples get into the boat and go ahead of Him to the other side, while He sent the crowds away. [23] After He had sent the crowds away, He went up on the mountain by Himself to pray; and when it was evening, He was there alone. [24] But the boat was already a long distance from the land, battered by the waves; for the wind was contrary. [25] And in the fourth watch of the night He came to them, walking on the sea. [26] When the disciples saw Him walking on the sea, they were terrified, and said, "It is a ghost!" And they cried out in fear. [27] But immediately Jesus spoke to them, saying, "Take courage, it is I; do not be afraid." [28] Peter said to Him, "Lord, if it is You, command me to come to You on the water." [29] And He said, "Come!" And Peter got out of the boat and walked on the water and came toward Jesus. [30] But seeing the wind, he became frightened, and beginning to sink, he cried out, "Lord, save me!" [31] Immediately Jesus stretched out His hand and took hold of him, and *said to him, "You of little faith, why did you doubt?" [32] When they got into the boat, the wind stopped. *(Matthew 14: 22-32)*

Jesus was right there when Peter was ready to call out to Him. Not far away. He stretched out His arm. Jesus will always be there when you are ready to realize you need Him. He is never far away, out of earshot or reach. He knows when you are finally going to realize you need Him. Reach out.

WHAT IF?

If, what *if*? A favorite teacher of mine tried to instill in her students to ask, "What IF?" Basically, she was teaching us to *think it through.* When you catch yourself saying, "*if only I had,*" or "*if things were different*", after the fact, it is because you did not stop and think something through. But what my teacher wanted us to learn was to weigh the consequences beforehand. God's word has many *ifs,* too many to address in this short devotion. Consider:

> **IF** My people, who are called by My name, will humble themselves and pray and seek My face and turn from their wicked ways, **then** will I hear from heaven and will forgive their sin and will heal their land.(*2 Chronicles 7:14*)

IF = THEN. That is a cause and effect statement. Throughout the Bible God says that *if* we do something, *then* something will happen. Society has forgotten there are consequences. God expects us to *think* through, to be responsible, and to understand consequences. This was one of my favorite object lessons in classes at the high schools where I worked. There were teenagers following the crowd, the media, even Hollywood without thinking. They were not thinking for themselves. **IF** only parents would teach them to *think situations through,* in scenario form. **THEN** maybe they would make wiser choices. Of course, I was not allowed to **teach** Biblical morality. But, I could teach them to think.

In fact, I was encouraged to engage students in thinking as part of my job. In almost every class sometime during the day, students would get into a *current issues* debate. I could not instigate the debate or state my views unless specifically asked I could however, interject "What If?" That simple question would always get them thinking. Their first question back would always be, "what if *what*?" At this point I have them look at both sides of the discussion and ask them "what is the consequence?"

A few examples from some of the classes show you how we started. The discussions were much longer of course and they really had to think out why they believed what they believed:

- Abortion?
- *Is there a god; one god?*
- *Is Jesus God?*
- *Premarital sex?*

Discussions on consequences made kids think. I started my kids when they were as young as two years old. Asking themselves, "what if" helped them as pre-teens and teens to handle peer pressure and to think on their feet. It will help them as adults to make important decisions, especially when satan* is making everything gray, obscuring the truth. Instead of seeing my toddler about to make a wrong decision and yelling, "Don't". I tried to use our Heavenly Father's model, **"If, then."** Obviously, I am not talking about when they are about to reach for a hot curling iron, are touching a sharp tool, or doing anything dangerous. I think God sends through the Holy Spirit a loud "Don't" at times. It is important to instill in them the ability to reason, to question, to make good decisions and to think on their feet. Exactly the same way God teaches us as we grow in our Christian life. I would look at my girls and tell them they could decide like a big girl. Then I told them the consequences of the two choices, *if and then*. Then allow them to choose. Seldom did they want the punishment choice.

Just like God does with us, we can be used to help others make good decisions too. Maybe our kids, or children we work with; maybe teens, college and young adults, work associates, family or friends. Make them aware of their actions. Challenge yourself and others to realize, "*If* I continue to not listen and to disobey God, *then* I will suffer the consequences by my own choice. *If* I obey, *then* I reap the good consequences. And, like little children like to please their parent, I love knowing when I am pleasing God. Children like to know their parents are proud of them. We like knowing we are acting acceptable and according to God's will. Encourage others when they make good decision.

As an adult this should ring true in your life. Daily, we have decisions, choices. Sadly some we rationalize and make gray when they are not. God's word says, "*If, then.*" We have decisions to make and God has filled His Word with the wisdom we need to not make the wrong choice. When making those decisions. We sometimes, like children, choose to make wrong decisions regardless of guidance. We *choose* to disobey willingly and then whine when we receive the punishment.

We do not want the bad consequences of our choice but, made it anyway, why? *We chose*, not Him. He showed us in His Word what would happen. God's word says in Isaiah 5 woe be unto you when you make wrong choices. Wrong choices are sin. Sin separates us from God..

> Woe to those who call evil good, and good evil; Who substitute darkness for light and light for darkness; Who substitute bitter for sweet and sweet for bitter! *(ISAIAH 5:20 NASB*

Do you have a decision to make today? Talk it out. Maybe it is a decision you can talk out in front of a child or young person. Use it as an opportunity to teach others how to decide. Take every opportunity to show others and let them watch you asking yourself, "what if I am wrong?" … 'what if I am right?"

*satan – I know people capitalize the "S" but, I do not. I refuse to give him any status of importance. He is a snake, so satan, devil, etc. are lower case, as he is one.

PICK YOUR BATTLES

The mom said in exasperation to me, "I am just picking my battles". Is that what God is asking parents to do? Pick the battles? Are not all battles *His*? Which means the victor is decided, so why not fight the battle? By picking your battles are you not just really choosing which ones not to fight? That is really just leaving them for satan* to claim without a struggle. This is your child you are talking about, not somebody else's and certainly not satan's* (although I have heard parents say their child is the spawn of satan* in jest. What a sad commentary on your home.)

> *Acts 9:1-21: God turned Saul into Paul. Saul saw Jesus. Paul praised Jesus. Jesus brought change.*

There is no child that cannot be made into a child of God by Jesus. Show them Jesus in you. Be careful what they see, hear, and say. It is a parent's job, not the churches, not the schools. Schools and churches can only reinforce. If God made you a mother or a father, then be the parent; *parents* decide. You do not lord over your kids; however, you set the parameters, the borders in which they live their lives. You cannot *pick* battles. They are all battles that God has won. If something they are doing is really bothering you then sit them down and tell them what it is, why it is wrong and why it is not going to be allowed. Do not wave it off because you do not want to *fight that battle*. Realize that the thing that is bothering you is the Holy Spirit telling you to be the parent. Here are just a couple of examples I have encountered over the years:

1. A Mom comes into the Christian bookstore where I am working. She says her daughter wants music by Hip-Hop/Rap artists. She

says she does not know what to do. She hates the music, cannot understand it, and does not want it in their home. She says she hopes the words are okay; it is hard to understand and is so loud. Then she says, "What am I to do? I have to pick my battles."

2. Another mother walks in with her preteen and teen daughters. Mini shorts would be longer on these girls. Cheeky is an understatement. She sees the eyes of women around her and sighs, "What's a mom to do? At least I know where they are. You must pick your battles".

Neither of these moms is picking their battle, nor are they parenting. They simply do not want confrontation. The truth is, if Jesus is not seen in their child, they have handed the battle over, that Jesus has already won, to satan*. If the *message* cannot be discerned in the music, if it cannot be understood, then it is just noise. If the appearance is not modest, if it implies you are anything but a Christian, then it is not for your daughters. Sons can be immodest in dress as well.

You *cannot* pick your battles. You can choose what *is* a battle. The Holy Spirit will let you know where to draw the line. Ignoring it is *not picking your battles.*

Problems arise when parents do not set boundaries. When they are little you teach them to dress as Christians; modesty is taught early on in their life. That does not mean they are in long robes, unfashionable, etc. It means, you teach them their Christian character must show through the clothes. When my girls were toddlers, I would lay out clothes for the day from which they could choose. They did not pick pj's to wear to church (as I have seen done) simply because those were not within the boundaries for that day. When they were old enough to help choose the clothes they wanted to wear, I would scout out the store if possible, beforehand. If not, as we walked through, I would point out areas they could choose from. When they started wearing makeup, they were taught that if someone says, "nice eye makeup, love the eyeliner, or nice lipstick," instead of, "you look nice", then they had on too much of the item.

In other words, making something stand out overwhelms the total person. They never wore words on their backsides. Never understood why parents would want everyone walking by to stare at their daughter's backside. Just think about it. And allowing them to draw attention to cleavage and other body parts might be the fashion but not God's. The current fashions include showing your boxers, your bras, and bodylines. Now those are battles! God holds you responsible for your child's testimony. There is no way that people are looking at your child and thinking wow look at that testimony for Christ when they are dressed inappropriately. If their appearance causes lust, you are responsible before God. Women and their daughters baring cleavage, cheeky thighs or, anything that would cause a man to stumble in church is beyond any reasoning. Dressing like the world in the world is not a testimony. So then how can you bring the world's dress into God's house? How are parents going to stand before God and say, "I was just picking my battles? Attending Christian functions, worship and services in immodest clothing is against God's Word. It is your job to teach your son and daughter to walk, talk and look Godly, not worldly; and you should be doing this by example as well. Kids can be very fashionable within parameters set by His word. They do not need to be social outcasts. Parents that succumb to their kid's dress wishes, music wishes, and curfew wishes have long ago allowed the child to become the parent. Taking back your role as parent will not be easy, battles never are. Jesus won that battle, ask Him how to proceed.

> …that you would walk in a manner worthy of the God who calls you into His own kingdom and glory. *(1 Thessalonians 2:12 NASB)*

> Therefore I, the prisoner for the Lord, urge you to walk worthy of the calling you have received, [2] with all humility and gentleness, with patience, acceptingone another in love…*(Ephesians 4:1-2 HCSB)*

*satan —still a snake, so satan, devil, etc. are lower case, as he is one.

ROOTED

The other day I wrote down this thought on my Mom2Mom Christian Parenting Facebook page:

> "With God all variables are just possibilities
> in the scenario." Renee' Green....

It is true. All the variables in our lives are possibilities in God's hands. He uses them to mold us and shape us into His perfect plan for us. We have a habit of messing things up. We try to plant ourselves where and how we think we should be at any given time. We make our lives comfortable and God must make us uncomfortable to get us back where we need to be.

Life has a way of redirecting the streams that feed us. Sometimes we end up in a desert place. Circumstances can make it seem that the water has redirected out of reach or gone underground too deep to reach. That is when and where we find out how we are rooted.

Roots make a difference. The Redwood trees are the grand trees, towering above all others. Yet their root system is shallow and should not support the mighty trees. The secret to their strength is that they tie in with their fellow Redwood trees and are linked together in an underground system. They are strong from the little seedling to the oldest tree in the forest. They share their roots, their nourishment. The ones furthermost from the streams and lakes are nourished through shared roots by the trees near water.

As Christians, we connect with our family and fellow Christians through churches and prayer groups. We support and nourish each other. We are never alone. We intercede in prayer for each other. We encourage and lift each other up even if the circumstances we are going through have left us feeling like we are way out in the desert. God uses the variables in our lives as possibilities to make us strong if we allow Him to use them. He will bring fellow Christians alongside us to aid in our trials as well as in our growth.

Country singer Tanya Tucker sang a song many years ago with these lyrics in the chorus:

> "There's a tree in the backyard that never has been broken
> by the wind. And the reason it's still standing is it was
> strong enough to bend."

Sometimes storms come and threaten to destroy us. Our roots are strongly anchored, but the winds are threatening to crack and break our limbs and level us to the ground, leaving us useless, leaving us just roots with no visible life. During these storms we need to be bendable; rooted, yet strong enough to bend. Life kicks up some mighty strong winds. Are we willing to bend as He allows the winds to blow? Or, do we stiffen' up and fight back, as though we can change the storms of life. Can you thank Him for the storm, rain and wind that ultimately make you strong? Do you keep your roots attached during bad weather to your underground network, allowing others to be blessed by interceding on your behalf with Him? Or, do you give up and try to go it on your own?

Driving around you pass millions of trees you do not notice, but then there is that tree you pass that has character. It may be a little bent, or show signs of storm damage, yet it is strong and beautiful, producing fruit or flowers even though it is scarred by life's storms. You may even see its roots here and there showing its strength in its surroundings. While other trees will be cut down without opposition, *that tree*, it will be considered. It will be noticed and preserved, maybe even singled out as a center point for a park. It has survived, it has character, it is strong.

Today there are all kinds of variables facing you, many harsh. Will you thank Him, remembering that "all things work together for good"? Are you going to try to handle it all on your own? Will you reach out to family, even your children, to fellow Christians and secure your *roots*? Will you allow the variables to be the possibilities in His hands?

> Consider it all joy, my brethren, when you encounter various trials. *(James 1:3)*

> And we know that for those who love God all things work together for good, for those who are called according to his purpose. *(Romans 8:38)*

Shackled By A Heavy Burden

Come to Me, all of you who are weary and burdened, and
I will give you rest. ²⁹ All of you, take up My yoke and
learn from Me, because I am gentle and humble in heart,
and you will find rest for yourselves. ³⁰For My yoke is easy,
and My burden is light. *(Matthew 11:28-30)*

You know the days where all the burdens are so heavy, we feel we are going
to topple over under the weight? Right now I am heavy laden with a long
list.

There are so many clichés Christians use when going through hard times.
We tie them to scripture, halfheartedly believing them with our heads and
not our hearts. We sing songs like, *He Touched Me* and buy books, plaques,
and bookmarks to encourage us; which are all are well and good. Somehow
though, we do not get to the heart of the matter. None of these make the
burdens go away. Just because He is carrying the load, the problems, the
burdens, it does not mean they are gone. It means you trust Him with
your entire life, good and bad, and waiting on His time. The ill may or
may not be healed on earth, but they will be healed in Heaven if they are
Christians. That crisis you are in will resolve, in His time and in His way.
That job will come, in His time and in His way.

God did not let Abraham sacrifice Isaac, but He did allow him to place his
son on the altar and raise the knife. God took Abraham to the brink. Why?

Abraham knew God is sovereign and faithful; he trusted God. Sometimes we go down to the altar *kicking and screaming*, Oh, if we would only say:

> ,,,for I know whom I have believed, and I am convinced that He is able to guard what I have entrusted to Him until that day. *(2 Timothy 2:12)*

Sounds like the lyrics of a really good song does it not? We allow ourselves to believe with our heads yet not walk with our hearts as well. We are shackled because we talk the talk and do not walk the walk. All are clichés we speak if we are not careful. Some of us are like, *that's my burden and I'm sticking' to it!* Some wear their *thorn in the flesh* like a badge of honor, almost as though they are *proud to suffer* for God.

The truth is, *if* we could solve our own problems, we probably would not seek Him. The deeper the problems the more we *should* seek Him. We should seek Him every day in every way. But being the humans, we are, we sometimes need to go to the *brink of destruction* for no other reason than He wants to take us to another level of trust.

The way Abraham reacted to where God was taking him taught Isaac truths about God. Since Isaac was not kicking and screaming, I surmise that Abraham had long since been teaching Isaac to trust God no matter the circumstances. What do others see when we are asked by God to do a difficult thing or go through a difficult time? Are you shackled?

Scars are just well-built bridges to hold parts together, strong structures you can rely on from the past to carry you through the future.

You do not just stand there. They are meant to heal you, while holding you together, to help you move forward. Where are your bridges taking you?

Remember, Jesus showed them His scars *after* the resurrection. They did not hurt any more but, they all remembered when they looked on His scars. His scars were a bridge for us.

WHERE'S YOUR BAGGAGE?

My husband traveled all over the USA, Canada, Europe, and Asia. I could not count the many trips I made to the airport to pick him up. I arranged to meet him in baggage claim many times. As I waited, I watched people as they claimed baggage. It was quite entertaining. It is amazing what people will tote around. Baggage claim: if the luggage could talk, oh the stories they could tell.

There are **so** many bags:

- All shapes
- All size
- All weights

Some are:

- Worn
- Ugly
- Damaged
- Lost

Many people's lives are like baggage claim. They gather and carry on life's journey and it all just keeps getting heavier and heavier. And sometimes they lose part of themselves without even noticing.

A few years ago, when our son-in-law returned overseas, one of the bags he was carrying was lost. According to the airlines, it never left the airport here. Weeks went by and still no one found the bag.

The theory is the tag got torn off on the belt going down from the ticketing area to the sorting area for planes. It would have been thoughtful for the airport employee at the end of the belt to mark that bag with date, time, and belt. That could have helped locate the luggage, no one noticed. It is still missing. I think that is what happens when people's lives are so hectic, something goes missing and because they are so busy, no one notices.

Our daughter and granddaughters followed him weeks later with their baggage. I decided to treat their bags like I do packages here in the states. I typed up a very large piece of paper stating: *luggage belongs to and destination.* Each piece had their name and address on the outside, and on the inside I laid the paper on top before closing the bag. There was no doubt to whom they belonged. It was a way to keep them together. The lost bag ended up in a pile somewhere, long forgotten. The identified bags went home.

Unlike our traveling baggage, we often carry our life's baggage around daily. Piling it on day after day until weighted down we cannot function at all. Our tags get lost. No one knows who we are. All the regrets, the *what ifs*, and *only ifs*, they load us down. Maybe we feel it would be nice if our baggage tags were just torn off and our baggage was lost, forgotten. That just does not happen in real life. In the Christian life that should not happen. We just need our luggage clearly marked. Sometimes we set the baggage down only to hold on to the tickets and go back and pick it up later. We need to learn to label our baggage, inside and out, *Belongs to, destination: Jesus.*

Give Him your tickets and let Him carry your baggage.

Cast your burden upon the LORD and He will sustain you; He will never allow the righteous to be shaken. *(Psalm 55:22 NASB)*

Then Jesus said, "Come to me, all of you who are weary and carry heavy burdens, and I will give you rest. *(Matthew 11:28 NLT)*

What are you still carrying? You were never meant to bear your burdens. Give Them All To Jesus.

No Time Like The Present

Pandemic 2020 – Old satan* is up to his tricks. Because he has dominion, he thinks he is in control. I grew up in Christian and Missionary Alliance Churches (C&MA) founded by A.B. Simpson. He also wrote songs. One of my favorite's attests to God's promise and faithfulness:

> *"Yesterday, today, forever, Jesus is the same, All may change, but Jesus never—glory to His name! Glory to His name! Glory to His name! All may change, but Jesus never—glory to His name!"*

We ask God, can you fix this, make it like it was? We want Him like He has been in our past. We hope for what He will be in the future while ignoring Who He is in the here and now. Jesus is the same as He was in the past and will be in the future. Open your heart to Who He is in your present.

Church buildings are closed. Yet worship has not been stopped. God is the same. We can still pray. We can still thank Him. We can sing praises to His name and not only in our homes or cars. Worship is in our hearts, not in a building. We do not need sound and lighting systems in a theater setting. No lights, no sound systems, no drama actions, no theatrics, no emoting and suddenly we are back to simple worship, just like His creation.

1 Praise the LORD! Praise the LORD from the heavens; Praise Him in the heights! 2 Praise Him, all His angels; praise Him, all His *heavenly* armies! 3 Praise Him, sun and moon; praise Him, all stars of light! 4 Praise Him, highest heavens, and the waters that are above the heavens! 5 They

are to praise the name of the LORD, for He commanded and they were created. 6 He has also established them forever and ever; He has made a decree, and it will not pass away. 7 Praise the LORD from the earth, sea monsters, and all the ocean depths; 8 fire and hail, snow and clouds; stormy wind, fulfilling His word; 9 mountains and all hills; fruit trees and all cedars; 10 animals and all cattle; crawling things and winged fowl; 11 kings of the earth and all peoples; rulers and all judges of the earth; 12 both young men and virgins; old men and children. 13 They are to praise the name of the LORD, for His name alone is exalted; His majesty is above earth and heaven. 14 And He has lifted up a horn for His people, praise for all His godly ones, for the sons of Israel, a people near to Him. Praise the LORD. *(Psalm 148 NASB)*

God has intervened in modern services. Many had become praise oriented only, but they called it worship. I believe He is using the current pandemic circumstances to shake up these concepts and wake His church. I was raised on sound Biblical teachings and sound Biblical music. Everything from the front of the churches led worship of who God *is* with *humbleness and reverence.* Sunday mornings we worshipped. We went back on Sunday nights for praise and testimony. You cannot praise and give testimony for what God *does* until you worship Him for *who He is.*

Growing up in church we sang songs like A. B. Simpson's songs, based on scripture, not *feel good* to sing, *toe tapping* and *emotion raising* productions. The Biblical truths we sang aloud were not repetitive lines. We sang truths from God's Word that raised our spirits, no theatrics needed.

The song above that Simpson wrote was based on Hebrews 13:8. Jesus Christ is the same yesterday and today and forever. Now, over 100 years later, the hymn's Biblical truths are sung around the world in many languages.

May we live today with our feet on the solid ground of His promises because Jesus is the same; yesterday, today, forever.

What Is Missing?

I am reading, hearing, and seeing more and more topical sermons, studies, and programs on why so many are not attending church. There are lists on numbers declining and statistical findings; excuses for why people are not coming together with fellow believers in worship. God's Word instructs us:

> Not forsaking the assembling of ourselves together, as the manner of some is; but exhorting one another: and so much the more, as ye see the day approaching. *(Hebrew 10:25)*

Who are they?

- There are long time church members staying home.
- Families bouncing from church to church.
- Young people discouraged and looking elsewhere, even the world.
- Visitors that do not return. All searching, hungry, looking.

Why is this? I have not found the answer in any list I have seen. That is because the lists are based on excuses. The writers all focus on excuses, not the reason. The reason hits too close to home. Many of them are the cause. There is only One reason. He is missing.

This is not new. John wrote of churches in His day that were found lacking, where He was missing. Only two were positive, Smyrna and Philadelphia. 28-1/2% of the churches in his day were found faithful.

Sadly, too many of our churches in America today are becoming more like the other 71-1/2% written about in Revelation. This is the message John needed churches to hear and why God had it recorded. It is how churches are held to accountability. Many churches are a combination of more than one of the ones John wrote to; how tragic.

1. **Rev 2:1-7** Ephesus churches that have forsaken God as their first love
2. **Rev 2:12-17** Pergamum churches that need to repent
3. **Rev 2:18-29** Thyatira churches with false teachers/teachings
4. **Rev 3:1-6** Sardis churches have fallen asleep, simply exist, there is no visible life
5. **Rev 3:14-22** Laodicea churches that are lukewarm, fence straddlers, tolerate sin to keep peace

If only the flocks had shepherds (pastors, teachers, leaders) that pointed to The Great Shepherd and led in Worship. People are looking for worship. Only worship fills that nagging empty void. It is a place in us created by God for communion with *Him*, and *Him* alone.

And the void that was created by the fall of man can only be filled by restoration of communion with God. Consecrated, sanctified, and humbled by the great *I AM*, we can approach with our hearts now humble and reverent in worship of Him. That is the hunger everyone is yearning to be sated.

There is a time and place for praise and rejoicing for all He has done. But only after we have worshiped who He IS, the Great I AM, can we know how to praise Him fully. How can you adequately praise someOne you do not know who He is? You must truly, reverently and in all humbleness, bow your heart before Him. El Shaddai, El Elyon, Lord God Almighty, The Highest God.

We have a generation that feels they have worshipped God because they have praised Him. Through all the good feelings and emotional highs, the theatrics, lightings, gesturing and posturing they leave service fulfilled. It lasts until they get to the car or the restaurant and everyone starts grumbling. Diluted by the world being brought in to God's house, most have never been in a House of Worship. They will try and recharge themselves throughout the week by putting on praise songs, motivational speakers, and try to shout, clap and dance. Yet they feel empty shortly thereafter. They do not know how to worship the Great I AM, so their praise is unfulfilling. They put the proverbial cart before the horse and find no success in moving towards God. Time and place, *Ecclesiastes 3*.

Families move from church to church searching and trying different programs. Youth become delusion and leave. The elderly become hungrier for real worship they once knew. There is one reason church attendance is declining: no place to Worship, no reverence, no humbling, no teaching of El Shaddai, El Elyon. All the praising of what He has done can never replace who He is, the Great I Am.

Sometimes You Have To Drink The Cup

As I looked at the Good Friday scripture and all The Lord went through, my mind was drawn to His words:

> Father, if You are willing, remove this cup from Me; yet not My will, but Yours be done. *(Luke 22:42 NASB)*

As a human it was impossible, He wanted to be spared. But, as the Son of God it was possible. He had to drink the cup given Him to fulfill God's plan, God's will. Jesus had to go through every step, not skipping any, not taking an easier way.

How then should we expect an easier path if God intends us to go through a hard time? So many times, we just want it easier, smoother. But that is not what Jesus finished His prayer with. It is okay for us to ask for the cup we are handed to be removed. But lest we lose the blessing of the plan, we should finish with, "yet not my will, but Yours be done." How often do we miss the blessing by not willingly accepting His cup?

In June of 2015 I wanted the cup removed instantly. It was hard to ask for His will be done. My mind was not working completely as it was. But I kept asking for His help. Often discouraged, and confused, with fears for what would happen next, I kept alert for the next sip of the cup I was handed, one drop at a time. Patience eluded me at times. But The Comforter was always there to help with any momentary lapses.

In the months, following my subarachnoid and intracranial bleeding stroke, I went through a myriad of contemplations. I have short term memory loss, so I took lots of notes. I reread what I wrote many times in hopes of getting my thoughts on paper before I forget them again. Our brains are so complex. God gave us 100% of a brain and allows most of us access to only 10%. Can you imagine how mankind would wreak havoc if we could access all our brain? Super computers would not begin to describe them. It is no wonder God only allows us to access so little and that we come here as infants to grow into the knowledge our brain can achieve.

For me, part of my brain died. I have a lesion the size of your little finger in the front left lobe. I have been on a rollercoaster ride of unbelievable magnitude as I learn to maneuver through and around my damaged brain. I am brain damaged but, not brain dead. The part that died cannot be made alive. But so much more is waiting to be used by His grace. It reminds me of how I am to be dead to sin and not pick it up again. Grow and move on.

There were, and still are, some hurdles that felt insurmountable as I learned to access other parts of my brain for speech, strength, swallowing, and accomplishing daily tasks. Everything. I am is a miracle. Though part of my face feels numb and I have trained my throat to swallow without strangling; though my right side is weak, and tingling and my head has hurt for over six years, I am getting well. I function normally. I worked full time for two years before our office was closed. Now I still substitute teach. Each day I am better, stronger. One sip at a time, the cup was not taken from me nor given all at once. I have no doubt God could have made me whole instantly. He chose not to heal me instantly. My cup was full, and I had to learn to sip it slowly. I have grown with each sip.

Jesus took His cup. As Christians we will have cups if we are to become more like Him. Someday I may know how many cups I was spared, how many I refused, and the blessings I gained through the ones I accepted by His Grace.

LUKE 22:42 KJV
"...Father, if thou be willing, remove this cup from me: nevertheless not my will, but thine, be done."

One sip at a time. One step at a time.

Trust. Obey. The more you trust, the more you obey. The more you obey, the more you trust. Sips are like that.

Why Does God Whisper?

There is nothing like quiet. Do you ever stop and listen to a breeze? Sometimes I do, especially at the beach where it lifts the waves in an unbelievable, calming sound. Because I am an extremely outgoing type of personality, when I get quiet and listen for God's sounds in His creation, people think I am sick. It is not uncommon for me to be asked if I am feeling alright. When I am quiet, I am listening.

My husband and I relish in our time together when we are quiet. One time my daughter asked me if we were okay. I asked her what she meant. She said, "you and dad go to the beach together and he fishes or reads, and you shell, but you never talk." We talk. We just do it without words. Sometimes, we sit and read for hours, or we go to the beach and he fishes, and I shell. I always look up and watch him reel in his fish. He looks out to watch me shell. If I get out of sight for too long, he comes looking to check on me. We communicate without words, many times. We have been married for forty-four years and we dated almost seven. We knew each other four years before we dated. That is fifty-five years of talking, even if we do not say a word. Through the years we have grown close enough to not always need to use words. I will be honest, sometimes we do miscommunicate. We are only human after all. We talk just the same, we communicate with or without words. We need not Shout to each other, or constantly talk out loud. With some relationships, quiet *is* conversation.

Our walk with the Lord is like that. God does not yell to us or shout from Heaven. Most of what He tells us is in a whisper. Why?

I KINGS 19:12 ESV
"And after the earthquake a fire, but the LORD was not in the fire. And after the fire the sound of a low whisper."

There is a story of an old preacher who is visited by a young man in trouble. He tells the preacher he has prayed and prayed, and God has not answered. The old preacher says something. But the young man could not hear him, so he moved closer, "what did you say?" The preacher repeats it, and again the young man moves closer, "What? I cannot hear you." One more time the old preacher repeats himself and the young man walks right up to him and asks him to repeat again.

> **"God sometimes whispers," he said, "so we will move closer to hear Him."**

My best conversations with *God* are when I say nothing at all.

> Then He said, "Go out and stand on the mountain in the LORD's presence. "At that moment, the LORD passed by. A great and mighty wind was tearing at the mountains and was shattering cliffs before the LORD, but the LORD was not in the wind. After the wind there was an earthquake, but the LORD was not in the earthquake. After the earthquake there was a fire, but the LORD was not in the fire. And after the fire there was a voice, a soft

whisper. When Elijah heard it, he wrapped his face in his mantle and went out and stood at the entrance of the cave. Suddenly, a voice came to him and said, "What are you doing here, Elijah?"*(1 Kings 19:11-13 HCSB)*

This you know, my beloved brethren. But everyone must be quick to hear, slow to speak...*(James 1:19 NASB)*

PECK-A-LITTLE, TALK-A-LITTLE

There is a scene in the musical *Music Man*_when all the women start chattering like a passel of hens. They were bent on telling the *Music Man* about the librarian. There was probably a little truth in what they said, but mostly it was their jealousies and need for gossip that spewed from their mouth. We laugh when we watch the scene.

Gossip is not new, it has just changed styles. Since the introduction of cell phones, gossip has gone global. No longer just in the neighborhood (or church foyer), gossips have worldwide reach through cell phones and via social media. Kids have used these various sites for bullying, and it is called cyber-bullying. Careless chatter goes out worldwide never to be retrieved. Words hurt, they scar and sometimes those scars ruin lives. It does not matter if you are talking behind someone's back or to their face; words once out cannot be taken back. Like the toothpaste squeezed out, you cannot make it go back in the tube.

Whether working or shopping, or maybe at the park or beach, you hear so much you wish you did not have to hear. People's private lives are spilled out into the air as people wander around chatting on their phones. Conversations best kept private are spilled out over aisles. It seems people think they are in their own private phone booth and because no one is on the aisle with them, in their mind at least, then no one can hear them. And of course, there are those that think they must shout their words across the phone for it to get to the other end of the line.

People just like to talk. In specific they like to *peck a little* at others; it makes them feel better about themselves to tear others down. Once started their *talk-a-little* becomes *talk-a-lot.* The art of silence has gone, resulting in not listening. So much of what is being said anymore is actually heard. Our ears are in overload and you must get our attention.

Recently a father let a loud whistle in the store to get his kids to come. He looked at my stunned face as if to say, "what?" When his kids do not listen to their names or him talking, he resorts to whistling for them like a dog. He does not even know how sad that comes across.

Would it not be better to really *pick little* to say, and *talk little* so that when you did speak others would want to hear what you say? Would there not be less hurt and less anger if people slowed down and chose their words carefully? God thinks so.

> Know this, my beloved brothers: let every person be quick
> to hear, slow to speak, slow to anger. *(James 1:19 ESV)*

Nobody's Business

What Are You Telling The World Around You?

From time to time we try to go to the beach to enjoy peace and quiet and unwind a little. We choose a beach that is 'smoke free', has a lifeguard (keeps the noise down of wild partying) and one that has great fishing and shelling. Yesterday when we arrived there were less than 1/2 dozen people on the beach. We settled in about 10 feet from shoreline for the view. The birds were singing, waves lapping, and a nice gentle breeze had the trees whispering.

That lasted maybe an hour before a woman settled in between us and the shore. I never have understood why when there is a whole couple of football fields of beach to choose from, people set right down on top of you. She not only was blocking the view, but she proceeded to light a cigarette up on the smoke free beach which meant we had to ask her to put it out. The signs are everywhere, however, we are the bad guys? She accused me of being the beach police. These beaches help people and children with respiratory illnesses, cancer, allergies and more. Then her friends showed up to give her some beers, on the alcohol-free beach, which is also on the six signs she passed walking to the shore. The friends did not stay long so she was left with her beer and nothing to do with her hands but use the cell phone. She pulled out her cell phone and began to talk and drink her beer. The more she drank the louder she became. The beach had added a few more families by this time but, she did not mind her conversations or language around these small children. Her business became everyone's as we had no choice but to listen to all her personal calls to her friends.

I do not understand why people forget that when they are in public talking on their phone, others are listening, even if they do not want to. Her first call began with her congratulating her friend on being added to the list of 'his exes'. Evidently children were involved because she continued to tell her to explain to them, they were a 'dysfunctional family'. The details she exposed us all to were unbelievable. She continued down her list of friends to call and went over a myriad of soap opera scenarios. This woman was probably in her late 50's or early 60's. You would think she would know better than to 'air the dirty linen' as our generation was supposedly taught. I am sure I will be accused of stereotyping, but you can just see this woman in her living room with her beers, cigarettes and tabloids while watching her soaps. All these reference materials make her highly qualified to be handing out advice it seems.

There is a time and place to discuss situations and none of those involve strangers. Talk shows and yellow journalism have done away with any sense of discretion. They have coined phrases to use as crutches like "dysfunctional" and "ex". The generation being raised in the shadows of all these public disclosures are being so conditioned and desensitized to sinful lives that they are not going to know sin when it slaps them. Sadly I know church goers with the same condition of talking out loud about anything, anywhere.

God says we are to guard our speech and our minds.

> Set your minds on things above, not on earthly things.
> (Colossians 3:2)

Parents, grandparents, teachers, and church leaders need to teach our children about guarding their minds and their speech so that when they are grown it will be automatic. We have become a world of gossiping and everyone believes they have the right to know each other's business as well as share theirs.

The good person out of his good treasure brings forth good, and the evil person out of his evil treasure brings forth evil. [36]I tell you, on the day of judgment people will give account for every careless word they speak, [37]for by your words you will be justified, and by your words you will be condemned. *(Matthew 12:35-37)*

What business are you sharing?

HOT, HOT, WATER

There is no author noted for this analogy, but its truth is so profound that it needs to be shared. I have written many blogs on trials, but you can never hear this truth too many times.

The story goes: A young woman went to her grandmother and told her about her life and how things were so hard for her. She did not know how she was going to make it and wanted to give up. She was tired of fighting and struggling. It seemed as one problem was solved a new one arose. Her grandmother took her to the kitchen. She filled three pots with water. In the first, she placed carrots, in the second she placed eggs and the last she placed ground coffee beans. She let them sit and boil without saying a word. In about twenty minutes she turned off the burners. She fished the carrots out and placed them in a bowl. She pulled the eggs out and placed them in a bowl. Then she ladled the coffee out and placed it in a bowl. Turning to her granddaughter, she asked, "Tell me what you see?" "Carrots, eggs, and coffee," she replied. *She brought her closer and asked her to feel the carrots. She did and noted that they got soft. She then asked her to take an egg and break it. After pulling off the shell, she observed the hard-boiled egg. Finally, she asked her to sip the coffee.* The granddaughter smiled, as she tasted its rich aroma. The granddaughter then asked. "What's the point, grandmother?" Her grandmother explained that each of these objects had faced the same adversity, boiling water, but each reacted differently. The carrot went in strong, hard, and unrelenting. However, after being subjected to the boiling water, it softened and became weak. The egg had been fragile. Its thin outer shell had protected its liquid interior. But, after sitting through the boiling water, its inside became hardened. The ground coffee beans were unique, however. After they were in the boiling water, they had changed the water. "Which are you?" she asked her granddaughter. – Author Unknown

What happens when trials knock on your door, how do you respond? Are you a carrot, an egg, or a coffee bean? Trying days happen all the time. On these trying days, which are you? Are you the carrot that looks solid and strong? Yet life happens. Your world is turned upside down, so you wilt, become soft and lose all your strength? Or, maybe you are like the egg. Your shell is perfect in shape and color. Your heart is soft and fluid. But then the heat turns up. Circumstances begin to boil all around you. What happens after a death, or a betrayal? Maybe you lose your job and financial security, even your home, then what? What happens when suddenly the water is too hot? Do you become cracked on the outside and hardened inside? Do you smell like the sulfur in an overcooked egg?

As a Christian should you not be more like the coffee bean? The hot water still boils, but the circumstances do not change you. You change the water with a deep beautiful color and aroma. People are drawn near to you because of your boldness. When things get worst you get better and change all around you.

These are hard times. Maybe you have been through worse. Maybe you will go through worse. The darkest hours are just before the dawn.

> God is in the midst of her, she will not be moved; God will help her when morning dawns. *(Psalm 46:5)*

PRACTICAL LESSONS

For Children and New Believers

The Ten Commandments

The Greatest of These Is Love

Who is the Creator?

The Importance of You – What Makes them Special – Finding True Friends and Love

The Potter and The Clay

The Gold Miner -Refinement

Build Your House

How Will You Grow?

Money $ Money $ Money

THE TEN COMMANDMENTS

You shall have no other god's before me
You shall not take My name in vain
Remember to keep the sabbath holy
Honor thy father and thy mother
Thou shall not kill
Thou shall not commit adultry
Thy shall not steal
Thy shall not bear false witness (lie)
Thy shall not covet (envy)

Where did the gray areas come from? Are there gray areas in the Bible? Today we are taught to be politically correct and tolerant, there is no black and white; only gray. Living in today's worldview is a struggle. Often the world is more vocal in their life than the church. While the world agrees on some black/white issues like murder and stealing (although there is a movement in the West to accept stealing when in need), the majority of the Ten Commandments are blurred in the worldview. We must be guarded with truth at home, church and everywhere in-between.

Did you memorize the Ten Commandments to receive an award? I did. We need to get back to teaching the basics truths in churches. The Ten Commandments are Old Testament, and we are not saved by laws but, by His grace. Yet the New Testament and Jesus taught the Ten

Commandments. Jesus lived and talked by the laws. Jesus said in Matthew 5:17-18,

> "[17]Do not think that I have come to abolish the Law or the Prophets; I have not come to abolish them but to fulfill them. [18]I tell you the truth, until heaven and earth disappear, not the smallest letter, not the least stroke of a pen, will by any means disappear from the Law until everything is accomplished."

We live our lives under adherence to these laws by God's grace. We should teach the Ten Commandments by the way we live. Can you name the Ten Commandments and what they mean?

THE TEN COMMANDMENTS

1. **Do not worship other gods** – What do others see as your *gods*? In other words, what is your priority?
   - Is it self? Do mom and dad's needs come before God or children?
   - Career? Are you the workaholic whose main priority is to climb the corporate ladder?
   - Money? Are you consumed with prestige and beating out the Jones, Smiths, and Rockefeller's?
   - Sports? Are you living for the gym or sports team, skipping worship for the gym, golf, sports game?
   - Clothes? Do you have to have the latest clothes, styles, shoes, hairstyle, manicure, and pedicure? Do you spend more time on your appearance then in your quiet time?
   - Family? Do you put your spouse and children before God? Do their wants and desires usurp His place in the family? If you allow this, then you are placing them first.

Other *gods* means anything or any person that is placed ahead of God. Often things are not bad in themself, it is where you place its priority, what you sacrifice to get it. Jesus showed this when dealing with satan* tempting Him:

Jesus said to him, "Away from me, satan! For it is written: 'Worship the Lord your God and serve Him only.'(*Matthew 4:10*)

2. **Do not worship idols** – The first commandment is about your priorities. The second commandment deals with your understanding of who God is and how to worship Him.
   - What do others see you use to form your view of God?
   - The Israelites wanted visual interpretations, idols, images to help them to worship God.
   - God says He wants us to worship Him, not through a speaker, preacher, musician, item or book.

There are those that hold sacred a symbol, the Cross, a WWJD item, a picture, etc. However, *satan has become much more subtle. What are you showing others to worship or allowing them to worship? Do you lift up a certain speaker? There are those that take a speaker and/or their message and make it their *word*. God is too big to be confined in all the speakers of the world. You must get to know Him through one on one time with *Him*, not vicariously through conferences, speakers, books. These are great tools; however, they are not a substitute for your time alone with God. You need time alone with God and others living with you should see your example. Too many are allowing the tools to form theirs and others' relationship with God. When human eyes are on a tool or messenger and not the message, then when those fail or fall, their view of God is damaged. What is your view being formed by? Some are focused on a musical group How often to you hear someone, yourself included, leaving a service, conference or concert and the conversation is all about the speaker, singers, or instruments? When you leave a time of worship and what is on the tip of your tongue is *not* the *message* but, the *messenger*, you are worshiping idols. Certainly it is okay to talk about the messenger, but too many times it has become the only focus and the message is lost. Sadly, there are many *groupies* of speakers, preachers and musicians who put the messenger over the message. Jesus said:

Yet a time is coming and has now come when the true worshipers will worship the Father in spirit and truth, for they are the kind of worshipers the Father seeks. *(John 4:23)*

3. **Do not misuse God's name** – We all think we are careful with this one.
   • Are we? We hear His name taken in vain in profanity daily.
   • Sometimes is in personal conversation
   • other times it is in a TV show
   • a movie, or a book.

Are you willing to walk away from a conversation? Will you ask someone not to use His name in vain? Would you change the TV show, leave the theater, or close the book? Others are watching. Do you know what the later part of this verse says?

You shall not misuse the name of the LORD your God, for the LORD will not hold anyone guiltless who misuses His name.*(Exodus 20:7)*

Is it possible to misuse His name in other ways than words uttered? We are CHRISTians. Do our actions, our way of life misuse His name? Jesus said:

But why do you call Me 'Lord, Lord,' and do not do the things which I say? *(Luke 6:46)*

4. **Keep the Sabbath holy** – The Hebrew word Sabbath, means *to cease, to pause or take an intermission*.
   • That means you take the Sabbath each week to rejoice in the Lord, celebrate His creation, and learn about Him.
   • It is not a day of *religious activities* and rituals.
   • It is a day of assembling in His house and meeting Him, receiving His message, and worshiping Him.

If others see you attend church to socialize, be seen, or as a duty, then you are not keeping the Sabbath holy. We all know that satan* loves to attack on Sunday. Anything he can do to keep us from going and/or get us grumbling. Sometimes it is just the social and entertaining value that keeps us from meeting the Lord on the Sabbath. God made this a commandment for our sake, for our relationship with Him. Jesus said:

> Then he said to them, "The Sabbath was made for man, not man for the Sabbath." *(Mark 2:27)*

5. **Honor your father and mother** – This commandment comes with a promise
   - Honor your father and your mother, that your days may be long upon the land which the Lord your God is giving you" *(Exodus 20:12.)*
   - For some reason many see this as a children's command. However, it was important to God to list it as a command.

This command and the following five are conduct, or behavior commands. When we teach to honor parents, we set a pattern of behavior for how to honor and worship God, and how to treat others including peers and elders. One does not cease to honor because they are older. For some it will mean physical care and support. But it always means to show respect, and to listen and learn from elders all your years. As adults we make our own decisions. And in cases where Christians do not have godly parents then they must follow God's guidance regardless of ridicule of un-saved loved ones. Look at the *big picture*. God is our Heavenly Father and we are to honor Him. We teach others that honor by showing honor to elders.

At His death, Jesus honored His mother and showed love and concern for her when He saw to her welfare after His death.

> [26]When Jesus saw his mother there, and the disciple whom he loved standing nearby, he said to his mother, "Dear woman, here is your son," [27]and to the disciple, "Here is your mother." From that time on, this disciple took her into his home." *(John 19: 26-27)*

6. **Do not murder** – We all feel safe here. However, we murder in our thoughts.
   - We watch things that make us insensitive to anger which is murder in our thoughts.
   - This commandment, like the fifth, is directed at our behavior.

Jesus said:

> [22]But I tell you that anyone who is angry with his brother will be subject to judgment. Again, anyone who says to his brother, 'Raca,' is answerable to the Sanhedrin. But anyone who says, 'You fool!' will be in danger of the fire of hell." *(Matthew 5:22)*

7. **Do not commit adultery** – Marriage is the foundation of the family.
- Our TV shows, movies, books, and magazines attack the ordination of marriage constantly. Here again is the big picture; Jesus is the groom, His church the Bride. No adultery, no divorce in that relationship.
- We need to show others God's plan for marriage based on His plan for our relationship with Him.
- You need to help others understand what the Bible teaches; even if you have found yourself, through choices of your own, not in God's plan for marriage, break the chain.
- For some you will have to explain the choices you made that were a wrong: choice of spouse, alcohol, drugs, money. Whatever got you off the plan God had for you own up to that bad choice.
- Or, if you came to Christ after those choices, you need to make a conscious decision to teach others the consequences of wrong choices.
- For others, it means you will select different TV shows, movies, books, etc.
- Do not desensitize others to adultery by exposing it to them daily. You are subconsciously giving them your acceptance.

God does not accept adultery in your relationship with Him, or in our relationships on earth. Jesus says you are guilty even if you do not commit the act. Do not kid yourself and think just because you have not acted on your thoughts that you are not guilty. Our actions begin in our minds.

> But I tell you that anyone who looks at a woman lustfully has already committed adultery with her in his heart. *(Matthew 5:28)*

8. **Do not steal** – Here again we think we are safe.
   - We have not robbed a bank or store. So we are not thieves in our minds.

There are little ways we show others that stealing is okay. And we all know that they can turn that into something bigger.

   - From cheating on taxes
   - Taking home work supplies

I thought I would focus instead on how we steal from God. We take time, possessions, family, and other blessings and make them *ours* instead of being stewards over what He has given us. Our time can be a large area of theft from God. We never give even 10% of our time back working for Him. Our money is often a huge area of theft from God. You cannot take from God His tithe without loss of blessings. Do we honestly give 10% or do we rationalize what the amount is that we are giving 10% of – pretax, gross, net, found money, inherited money? Possessions: Ever open your home up to visiting ministers, missionaries, youth groups, etc.? If you give 10% is that all you must give? How about your family and blessings, are those God's or yours? Would you give a son or daughter to ministry? Others are watching what we take from God and what we give back. Are we stealing from God? We take so much and give so little.

> What good will it be for a man if he gains the whole world, yet forfeits his soul? Or what can a man give in exchange for his soul? *(Matthew 16:2)*

9. **Do not lie** – I will not name names, but I can think of two incidences right now of Christians who rationalize sin.
   - One says that it is not a lie if you are going to tell them the truth eventually – in other words, you are just teasing them.
   - Another believes it is not a lie if it does not hurt anyone and something good comes from the lie.

Throughout the Bible we are told that God is truth, His way is truth, and His word is truth. God is pure. There is no gray area in truth. It is either truth or lie. The fact that you should not lie is a commandment tells you how important truth is to God. Catch yourself in half-truths, white lies, little exaggeration, fibs? Do not kid yourself, they are *lies*. Call them for what they are. If you do not, then you will be teaching others to lie, and one lie leads to another.

This character trait leads to other problems. Lying is a sin. We think of it as a small sin. There are no small sins. Sin leads to separation from God and even more sin. Soon your conscience is dulled, and you end up walking a life away from God. God does not like for us to tell lies. Jesus said:

> But I tell you that men will have to give account on the day of judgment for every careless word they have spoken. *(Matthew 12:36)*

10. Do not covet – Covet is want or desire. In our materialistic world is it any wonder we hear people say *I want* more than many other phrases?

- We rush to the store to get the latest in cars, clothes, phones, TVs showing others to covet.
- God says He will give us our needs, not our wants.
- Somewhere we decide it was a right to have our wants as well.

There is nothing wrong with material things until they fall into the category of the First Commandment. They have become our gods, our priorities. We circle back to the beginning of the Commandments. We set a standard for ourselves and others to suffer. There are instances where both parents need to work. However, if you are working to obtain things and an easier more prosperous life at the sacrifice of raising the children God has given you, then you are breaking the First Commandment. If we covet anything it should be to be more like Him. Covetousness is the root of many of the other sins. Someone covets and it leads to a lie, adultery, theft, or murder. We should not focus our lives on wants.

> [25]"Therefore I tell you, do not worry about your life, what you will eat or drink; or about your body, what you will wear. Is not life more important than food, and the body more important than clothes? [26]Look at the birds of the air; they do not sow or reap or store away in barns, and yet your heavenly Father feeds them. Are you not much more valuable than they? [27]Who of you by worrying can add a single hour to his life [28]And why do you worry about clothes? See how the lilies of the field grow. They do not labor or spin. [29]Yet I tell you that not even Solomon in all his splendor was dressed like one of these. [30]If that is how God clothes the grass of the field, which is here today, and tomorrow is thrown into the fire, will he not much more clothe you, O you of little faith? [31]So do not worry, saying, 'What shall we eat?' or 'What shall we drink?' or 'What shall we wear?' [32]For the pagans run after all these things, and your heavenly Father knows that you need them. [33]But seek first his kingdom and his righteousness, and all these things will be given to you as well. [34]Therefore do not worry about tomorrow, for tomorrow will worry about itself. Each day has enough trouble of its own. *(Matthew 6:25-35)*

*satan – I know people capitalize the "S" but, I do not. I refuse to give him any status of importance. He is a snake, so satan, devil, etc. are lower case, as he is one.

THE GREATEST OF THESE IS LOVE

How to make friends and find real love.

A simple visual on learning to love.

You begin making friendships from your early years in nursery, preschool, children's church and neighborhoods. As you interact with siblings and relatives you develop patterns of friendships from how they make friends. All the relationships in our lives will be built on love at some level. Scripture tells us *love* one another:

> [34]A new command I give you: Love one another. As I have loved you, so you must love one another. [35]By this all men will know that you are my disciples if you love one another. *(John 13:34-35)*

WHAT YOU NEED:

- Heart shape – they can make one (see picture below) or you can provide
- Words from 1 Corinthians 13 on pieces of paper
- Write (or let them make) the four words: Friendship, Physical, Spiritual and Mental (spelling lesson too!)
- tape/glue

<u>WHAT YOU WILL DO</u>:

1. Read the scripture to them, 1 Corinthians 13
2. Have them cut out the words, write the words referring to LOVE
3. Have them make a heart or give them one you have made

Divide the heart into the four areas and label

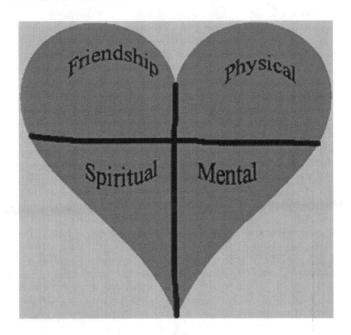

Place a hole in an area that has a problem. Too many holes will break the heart.

4. Talk to them about the words from 1 Corinthians as you talk about the four areas using the text below

Sadly many are not taught at home and at church about friendships, love, relationships, and looking for Mr./Mrs. Right. Many are left to figure love out on their own. It is something that affects their entire life whether they are a Christian or not. When you are not taught about something at home, someone else will teach you. There are movies, magazines, and books all dealing with relationships, friendships, marriage, and worldly views of love. Because the media throws the word love around and makes it synonymous with sex, many have no idea of what makes a friendship let alone a relationship or what they want in a marriage.

As Christians we have the answer straight from the manual. Have you really considered God's word and what He has taught about love? Everything you need to know about these different aspects of relationships is taught in 1 Corinthians 13. What is Love? How do you apply it as you grow so you know what you are looking for when it hits you? *(Please read note at end.)*

- *Love is patient*
- *Love is never jealous*
- *Love is never boastful*
- *Love is NOT a game*
- *Love is never proud*
- *Love is never rude*
- *Love is never selfish*
- *Love is never quick-tempered*
- *Love never holds a grudge*
- *Love loves the truth*
- *Love is saddened by evil*
- *Love is supportive*
- *Love is hopeful*
- *Love is trusting.*

This is love. Think about each area and apply them to whatever phase you are in; learning to make friends, dating, or searching for the perfect will of God in their life mate. When a child is learning about making friends they are learning the same thing they will need as they date and when falling in love. Basic truths must be consistent to have value. They cannot change with age. As adults we are watched to learn how we love. All of us can improve in that area.

I passionately believe that there are four areas that apply to making friends, relationships and ultimately in marriage. You need to balance all four as equally as possible for successful relationships, friendships, and marriage.

Four Areas To Balance:

1. Friendship – every relationship should begin with friendship – of all the words describing love above, which one(s) would you place into friendship? I think you would like to claim all of them about a friend; that is what makes them a best friend.

2. Physical – there is a physical level of all relationships, whether just friends or someone you want to marry. You must be comfortable with their physical presence – as they change over time, age, fade physically, or an accident or illness sets in, none of that will matter if you accept them as God made them. You learn that skinny, fat, short, tall, braces, it does not matter. Then, when you are older and looking for a lasting relationship, you are drawn to someone regardless of physical flaws. Then when dating, and chemistry sets in, the relationship is not lopsided. Chemistry can fade, a relationship built only on hormones will fail (learn this truth.) Physical is not just about being *hot* or *fine*. Everywhere you look you see couples that in the human eye look *lopsided*. And you think, "How did he/she get them?" They have found the true physical balance that real love is about.

3. Spiritual – you have a spiritual concern for this person as a friend; you have a spiritual bond with them in a relationship. If you are on two different wave lengths it will not work out. I am not allowed to talk about 'spiritual' matters at schools. I can only tell them that if they do not agree spiritually, like both are atheists, both environmentalists, both same theology, same beliefs, like faith, then they are bringing problems into the relationship; major hurdles to be jumped and negotiated until they are gone or they destroy the relationship.

4. Mental – you must be able to communicate. Many men do not want women that are more intellectual, but it goes further than that. If one values the pursuit of education and the other scoffs at it their kids will receive mixed messages. One will say, go play, you are only young once while the other wants to give them educational goals and values. It is not just education, it is all things mental, and you must be on the same wavelength and have a

healthy respect for the other partner's intellect. Never should one joke about the other partner's intelligence.

Basically, you must be healthily balanced in all four areas. You take into a relationship as few problems as you can, because when you take them in, they are in until resolved and/or they destroy the relationship.

When it comes to dating and marriage, the Bible is explicit about Christians seeking Christians. It is hard to be 'best friends' with someone with whom you are not 'equally yoked' (2 Cor 6:14-18), even more so in a relationship or marriage. I would go so far as say you should not date a non-believer. This is referred to as *missionary dating*. The hope of leading them to Christ through dating is never a good idea. Do not tempt yourself into falling in love with a non-believer by dating them.

By learning the scriptures about love and what the four areas are, you learn what you need for when making the all-important decisions in dating and marriage. When starting dating that should not be the first time you have thought about such matters or considerations. Give yourself the greatest gift, the ability to love as Christ loved us. The greatest of these is *love*.

*If you have not already started praying for your child's future husband/wife, then start now. I started when my girls were infants. If children are already teens, get busy praying. I assure you that satan** is not waiting in his planning on making a mess of things.

**satan – a lower case not worthy of an upper case.

WHO IS THE CREATOR?

The Creator – God Omnipotent

This is one of my all-time favorites and so easy and inexpensive object lessons. Depending on the age group you can make this as simple as, *God Made You* to *There is no way evolution is possible, God is Omnipotent and the Creator.* After they try to create, you can walk around the yard or the local park and really look at things (it is great if the little ones have those plastic magnifiers.) Help them see the wonder of creation and not just take it for granted. Show them how awesome their Creator is and all that He did in creating them.

What you will need:

1. Small pack of colored clay strips: You can go into any party store or superstore party-ware aisle where they sell inexpensive favors and pick up the mini pack of clay that comes in four little strips of varying colors.
2. Placemats to work on: You can use wax paper, pieces of cardboard or any washable surface.
3. Plastic fork, spoon and or knife (for designing and carving.)

Sit down at a table with everyone and make something, anything. Talk about how God created everything in the beginning. Talk about what a creator is and that truly the only real creator was God. Everything that any of you try to make will imitate something you have seen, so it is copied, not created. In truth man has never created anything but imitated everything from one of God's creations.

We are cloners at best. Many children try to make a unique animal as their own inventive, but it will have eyes (God made those), sometimes a nose, ears, many legs; they are copying. Everything we make is a copy of something in His creation. Even our computers are pitiful imitations of the way the brain works.

Kids are exposed to evolution at school. They need to be guarded with the truth. If they have been taught about evolution, and depending on the child's age, ask them questions about how evolution is possible? Which came first, the blood or the heart? Which evolved first, lungs or ribcage, the skin or the muscles? Depending on what part of biology they have had, this will open their mind to how unbelievable it is for something to evolve from nothing. Explain that adaptation to environment and evolution are not the same thing. Help your child understand how marvelous and all-powerful God really is as they see that they can create nothing but can only, imitate everything that God created. Help them see that as part of God's creation we are to care for all that God created. Help them understand how truly special mankind is to God in that He made us in His imagine.

> God created man in His own image, in the image of God He created him; male and female He created them.
> *(Genesis 1:27)*

It is especially important that you seek resources and arm yourself with the truth. Liars from satan* have been armed with 'facts' to back up his teachings that are being taught to children everywhere they turn in the world. You cannot just tell them, because I said so, every time they are asking, especially when it deals with spiritual things. And sadly, saying, "because God says so and I believe it" does not always settle the inquiring young minds. I have found that the Focus on the Family site has many sources for help.

Your children are never too old to learn and they will never quit asking questions. Be armed.

*always the liar, satan is such a lower case and I will always denote his name as lower case.

THE IMPORTANCE OF YOU
WHAT MAKES YOU SPECIAL

A great lesson for the young and the young in Christ

The Baker – The Importance of Ingredients

You can learn and teach a valuable life lesson right in your own kitchen. Bake a cake from scratch. Not a box. No shortcuts this time.

<u>What you will need:</u>

- 1 1/4 c. flour
- 1 tsp. baking powder
- 1/2 c. butter
- 1 c. sugar
- 1 tsp. vanilla
- 2 eggs
- 3 TBSP cocoa (optional – if you want to make it chocolate)

<u>What you will do:</u>

- Preheat oven to 350 degrees
- Mix butter and sugar
- Stir in the vanilla
- Stir in eggs
- Slowly add flour baking powder (cocoa)
- Pour in 8x8 pan; bake at 350 for 25 mins

Icing for the cake: Chocolate

- Blend together in a small bowl until smooth:
- 3/4 cup Powder Sugar
- 5 Tbsp. cocoa
- dash salt
- 1 Tbsp. melted butter
- 5 Tbsps. milk (reg., almond or coconut

Have fun with this one and talk as you go.

<u>What you are teaching</u>:

1. Each ingredient is important to the recipe or the cake will not turn out.
2. Everything in life will makes us the person God wants us to become.
3. You cannot take the flour out of the cake or it will not be a cake. You cannot take Christ out of your life and be a Christian.
4. No one drinks vanilla it is bitter, just like the sorrows in our life, but it is still important to make the cake's flavor right.
5. The eggs are so important, they bind and hold things together, just like the love of God and family.
6. The sugar is the good times that we all enjoy and want more of, but too much will spoil the cake.
7. The butter makes the batter smooth and helps it to cook evenly just like the Word of God in our life.
8. And do not forget the baking powder or the cake will not rise. Without the instructions and guidance of older Christians in their lives they will not grow up to be the adult God wants them to become.
9. You can add the cocoa and make the cake individually flavored and that is all the circumstances in their life that make them who they are, unique and different unto their Creator.

Use your imagination in making it unique to each person's situation. You can use various scriptures through the process, too many to list here. That will be part of your learning. Researching the Word is so important to your own growth. Now, go arm yourself and others.

THE POTTER

A lesson for yourself, a child or new believer going through hard times.

You are probably familiar with the passages of scripture referring to God as the Potter and we are the clay in *Isaiah 64:8*. There are so many verses you can attach to this lesson and so many truths. One of my favorite examples is the one I wrote while teaching a Pioneer Girls group to make ceramic items for Mother's Day. You can use already poured ceramic pieces from a ceramic store, a plaster piece from a craft store (in this case an oven would be for example only and not needed for actual firing – so five minutes max), or raw oven clay to make pots, jewelry, picture frames or characters. Use your imagination based on your resources and knowledge of whom you are teaching so that they can use theirs.

There are four ways to teach this lesson:

1. I would encourage you to find a potter or ceramic painting store and try this lesson.
2. Or you can find a potter's wheel and structure the lesson around making a pot.
3. Use a recipe and make your own from an online tutorial. (*Or, make your own – see note at end.)
4. You can buy 'bake in the oven' clay at a store like JoAnn, Michaels, Hobby Lobby or online.

You will have to adjust the lesson depending on what product you start with. For teaching the concept I am using green ware from a ceramic shop.

Using a piece of green ware that has not been fired and still has the seam edges intact:

1. First each person will pick a piece; just as God selects people to work on through the Holy Spirit and come unto Him as His child.
2. Next, show how to scrape the seams down until the seams are smooth. This is how God begins to clean up our life from all its rough edges left by the world (which was the pots mold) we came out from. We are born with a sin nature. God is gentle but firm so as not to break us, just as each student must be with their own piece of ceramic.
3. Then begin to sand lightly until there are no more visible signs of the seams. God will send spiritual sandpaper into each life to remove all the traces of the world. (I often refer to some people as my spiritual sandpaper, in a loving way.)
4. Next the instructor places each piece in the kiln to be fired until it is hard. (Describe if off site.) The fire is just the right temperature so as not to cause the piece to explode.

   No temptation has overtaken you except such as is common to man; but God is faithful, who will not allow you to be tempted beyond what you are able, but with the temptation will also make the way of escape, that you may be able to bear it. (*I Corinthians 10:13 NKJV*)

In other words, nothing will ever be so bad that it will cause a person to lose their faith in Him. The *fires* in life that God allows us to go through will make us stronger, not cause us to explode.

5. At this time note that if a good job of cleaning was not done, then that dirt is fired into the piece permanently. That is why it is so important that we not ask God to stop *cleaning on us* too soon or make the fire *not so hot*. We should welcome the trials in our lives that help to clean us of our *dirt* and *grit*.

Consider it all joy, my brethren, when you encounter various trials, knowing that the testing of your faith produces endurance. [4] And let endurance have *its* perfect result, so that you may be perfect and complete, lacking in nothing. (*James 1:2-4*)

Once the piece is out of the kiln and cooled detail using paint, etc. to make it unique; just as God adds details daily to your life to make us a unique person unto Him.

For you are a holy people to the Lord, your God, and the Lord has chosen you to be a people for His own possession out of all the peoples who are on the face of the earth. (*Deuteronomy 14:2*)

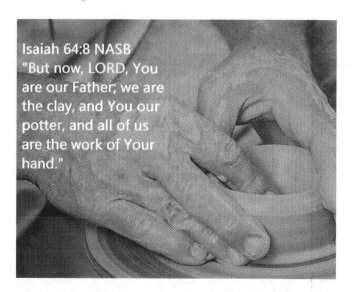

Isaiah 64:8 NASB
"But now, LORD, You are our Father; we are the clay, and You our potter, and all of us are the work of Your hand."

*You may want to make your own mold. An easy one is the globe. Take a tennis ball and cut out a small 'pouring hole' at the top. Cut the hole in half all the way through the ball until you have two equal halves. Wipe the inside clean. Put it back together using heavy rubber bands. You have made a mold. Pour a liquid molding substance called slip, or plaster of Paris, etc. into the mold. Keep checking for it to be setting up because you want to pour out the excess to leave it hollow. Let it sit overnight to dry even more. Remove the mold and let stand to air dry. With this mold you can do a World, a Light bulb, a head; many creative avenues using your imagination to adjust a lesson around the piece.

Use your imagination and encourage those you are teaching to use theirs. Remind them that nothing they can think of was not already created by God Himself. He is the Creator.

THE GOLD MINER

One of my favorite lessons is The Gold Miner. I made many trips to Dahlonega in North GA to go Gold mining. I have also ordered gold traced dirt and taught this lesson to Pioneer Girls and other youth groups in a classroom. The lesson can be adapted to any mining near you with a little imagination (ruby, sapphire, even shelling at the beach.) However, this can also be taught with sands and rocks (*see note below.)

The Gold Miner and the Importance of Fire

God has provided so many lessons and insight into Himself all around us. I would encourage everyone to try any availing mining attraction near them. There is so much to learn about God in our life through the experience.

You can order gold dirt online from companies like ConsolidatedGoldMines. com. Research near your area online.

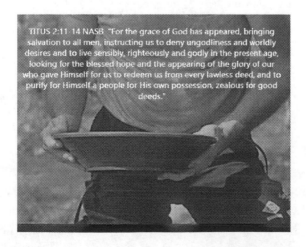

TITUS 2:11-14 NASB "For the grace of God has appeared, bringing salvation to all men, instructing us to deny ungodliness and worldly desires and to live sensibly, righteously and godly in the present age, looking for the blessed hope and the appearing of the glory of our who gave Himself for us to redeem us from every lawless deed, and to purify for Himself a people for His own possession, zealous for good deeds."

RENEE' BELLE ISLE GREEN

<u>What you will need:</u>

- Gold panning pan (pie pan, aluminum pie pan – simply score three 4" lines pressing in from outside 1/8" apart making sure not to puncture – see picture of pan above.)
- Large tub of water (this is best as an outdoor project.)
- Gold dirt or *you can use sand and some various sizes of rock (rice size to pea size) sprayed gold, some sprayed red (rubies) some sprayed blue (Sapphires) some silver/gold for fool's gold.

<u>What you do:</u>

- Place 2 cups of the gold dirt in the pan (*or sand and painted rocks.)
- Lower the pan just below the water

LESSON:

- God is the gold miner and the pan is Jesus.
- The dirt is the world we are living in as sinners and the water is the Holy Spirit at work in our life.
- The gold miner (God) uses his pan (Jesus) to separate the gold (us) from the dirt through the power of the water (the Holy Spirit.)
- The power of the water is just strong enough to not wash out the gold with the dirt. The pan has grooves scored in its side to make it possible for the gold to stay with the miner and not be washed away with the dirt, just like Jesus was scored with whips and scarred through nails and thorns and ultimately death, that we might have a way to God.
- Once the water (Holy Spirit) does its job, the scored pan (Jesus) saves the gold.
- The gold is spared, and now the miner (God) begins to prepare the gold. (At this point students just listen, their part is done)

The Holy Spirit works in our lives to bring us unto Jesus that we might be prepared by God to glorify Him. Once the Gold is separated out from the dirt by the pan and the water the gold miner starts the next process.

He submits the gold to fire to purify it from all the traces left by the dirt of the world, the hotter the fire, the purer the gold. The gold miner knows the gold is finished and totally pure when he can see his reflection in the gold. God continues to work in our life so that He might see Himself in us. We are totally purified when we reflect Him. When the miner (God) sees himself in the gold, it is purified.

Simple truths can be taught at any age by adjusting the story. Even if you are simply walking a shore looking for shells, you can teach someone the real treasures are buried and need to be washed to be found. Teach as little or as much as they can retain. Strengthen the faith of those you teach.

BUILD YOUR HOUSE

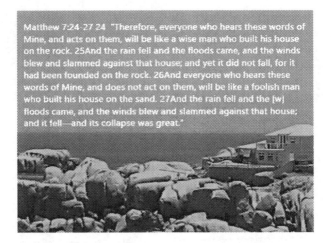

Matthew 7:24-27 24 "Therefore, everyone who hears these words of Mine, and acts on them, will be like a wise man who built his house on the rock. 25And the rain fell and the floods came, and the winds blew and slammed against that house; and yet it did not fall, for it had been founded on the rock. 26And everyone who hears these words of Mine, and does not act on them, will be like a foolish man who built his house on the sand. 27And the rain fell and the [w] floods came, and the winds blew and slammed against that house; and it fell—and its collapse was great."

Christians of all ages need to constantly be reminded of their spiritual house being built soundly on the Rock, our Lord. Music is a great way to teach Biblical concepts. Maybe you remember songs from VBS and children's church programs. One of my favorites was *The Wise Man Build His House Upon The Rock*. Another version, *Solid Rock*, by Mark Heard, is on the internet.

Based on these songs a lesson can be taught at home, or as a challenge at youth/college meetings. Scriptures: *Matthew 7:24-27*

What you will need:

- Large tub
- Water (gallon jugs of water or a hose if outside)

House #1:

- rocks – a slab stone or paver stone for base
- clay for mortar (or make your own mud allowing the structure to dry out for proper effect, a two-day, or week lesson for youth, one to build, one to come back and teach, watching results.)
- objects to use for door and windows, chimneys, etc. can made with plastic band rings from milk or orange juice jugs, plastic bangle bracelet, PVC connections, etc. (raid tool boxes and recycle bins,)

House #2:

- sand, and a cookie sheet or large aluminum pan for the house base to be built on
- rocks, tongue depressors, popsicle sticks, or cardboard for walls
- items for doors, windows, etc. as in House #1.

House #3: (Optional if you want to expand the lesson)

- rock for base
- sticks for walls (the concept here is the saved one that talks but not walks like a Christian.)

Songs: "The Wise Man Built His House" or "Solid Rock", by Mark Heard. Music helps us learn and remember.

THE LESSON:

Build a different house each day or all at once depending on time frame; time allotments and attention spans. As a group, it can be a one day, two-day or two-week project where they meet once each week (like a Wednesday. night group.)

Divide into groups as needed. It can be a challenge competition and timed as well. Work with what you need to accomplish. Let the building begin. You can talk as they build or interact in the building and wait until the water test to talk.

HOUSE: They are building a house on a foundation. The house is their Christian testimony, their life, their character in Christ. You can add to this part by adding in the Beatitudes from Matthew 5, also known as the *attitudes to be.*

ROCK:

Jesus Christ our Lord is the Rock; the foundation on which our Christian Character and testimony are built.

> he is like a man building a house, who dug deep and laid the foundation on the rock. And when a flood arose, the stream broke against that house and could not shake it, because it had been well-built. (*Luke 6:48*)

A good foundation is firm, deep. Building on anything else may be simpler but certainly will not last the test of time. So, they are building their life based on a right relationship with Christ, their Rock. They will face temptations and trials but because they are built upon the Rock, they will not be swayed by winds that bring the rains. There will be false teachers, people who teach things that are not in God's word. Yet they will not be swayed and tilted.

> 14 Then we will no longer be infants, tossed back and forth by the waves, and blown here and there by every wind of teaching and by the cunning and craftiness of men in their deceitful scheming. 15 Instead, speaking the truth in love, we will in all things grow up into Him who is the Head, that is, Christ. (*Ephesians 4:14-15 NASB*)

SAND:

Building on the sand are those that ignore the Lord, His teachings, and His will in their life. They rely on themselves and the world, its beliefs, and ideas. When trials, troubles and unfortunate circumstances arise, the sands shift and they become unstable, collapsing without support.

TWIGS: If you build the third house, on the rock, but with twigs, this is the house of the person that started off their Christianity and never yielded full control to The Lord. They never allowed God to build them up by reading the Bible, praying, and yielding their whole life to Him.

Once all the houses are built and ready for the water test, you can begin with a slow sprinkle and list things that come in life: Bad grades, broken toy, loss of a pet, breaking up of a friendship, loss of job, death of a love one, etc., based on their age and status in life. Increase the water flow. As the twigs and sand houses break apart, tell them that the water is the hard things in life like death of a family member, dad losing his job, someone being very sick, someone telling lies to them (relate what they are facing at this time in their life.)

The lesson learned: Without Christ as your foundation, the struggles of life will tear you down and destroy you. You must build your life each day on the solid foundation, the Rock, the Lord Jesus Christ and you must use His character to build the walls of your life so that when trials, temptations and troubles come, and they will, they will stand firm like their Rock.

People will tell you God will never give you more than you can handle. That is not in the Bible. The scripture says that He will not allow more than would cause you to lose your faith and that He will always make a way out. The way out is your foundation in Him, your faith. Lean on the power of the Holy Spirit who bears you up through all of life's trials. He is your escape.

> No temptation has overtaken you but such as is common to man; and God is faithful, who will not allow you to be tempted beyond what you are able, but with the temptation will provide the way of escape also, so that you will be able to endure it. *(1 Corinthians 10:13)*

How Will You Grow?

1 Corinthians 10:13

Lesson can be done anytime, anywhere and is a truth all Christians need to remember.

The Lesson: The Parable of the Sower

¹That same day Jesus went out of the house and sat by the lake. ²Such large crowds gathered around him that he got into a boat and sat in it, while all the people stood on the shore. ³Then he told them many things in parables, saying: "A farmer went out to sow his seed. ⁴As he was scattering the seed, some fell along the path, and the birds came and ate it up. ⁵Some fell on rocky places, where it did not have much soil. It sprang up quickly because the soil was shallow. ⁶But when the sun came up, the plants were scorched, and they withered because they had no root. ⁷Other seed fell among thorns, which grew up and choked the plants. ⁸Still other seed fell on good soil, where it produced a crop—a hundred, sixty or thirty times what was sown. ⁹He who has ears, let him hear."

John 15:5 NASB

"I am the vine, you are the branches; the one who remains in Me, and I in him bears much fruit, for apart from Me you can do nothing."

<u>What you will need</u>:

- A tray (can be a cardboard box lid, a storage lid, or even a trash can lid – anything you can spare)
- Small rocks, twigs/briars, potting soil
- Flower or vegetable seeds

<u>What you will do</u>:

- Poke tiny holes in bottom of tray for drainage.
- Mark box to make three areas
- Area #1 sprinkle some seeds
- Area #2 place a few rocks, a little dirt some twigs/thorns/briars and a few seeds
- Area #3 Cover area with soil and a few seed
- Water #2 and #3
- Set outside in a settled area where the lesson will not be blown away, but it will still receive .sun

Over time #1's seeds should blow away or be eaten; #2 and #3 should sprout but #2 should wither and die while #3 thrives.

<u>What you will teach</u>:

1. Going through life carefree without concern and no substance for growing in the Lord will destroy them (salvation but, no prayer, no reading the Bible, no fellowship.)
2. Going through life attending S.S., church, Christian camps but never having a personal relationship with Christ will also destroy them,
3. Going through life with proper nutrients, water, and sun will give them Life everlasting through His Holy Word the Bible (nutrients), Salvation/Baptism (water) and Son Jesus Christ (sun.)

As the process grows, you can talk with them daily as they observe the changes. Relate how changes in their life come when they walk close with the Lord. Without staying connected to the Vine, Jesus Christ, you will wither and die. You will not grow and show Fruit of the Spirit. There will be no sowing and planting seeds of the Gospel.

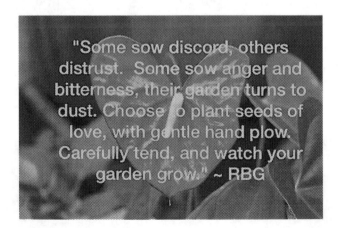

"Some sow discord, others distrust. Some sow anger and bitterness, their garden turns to dust. Choose to plant seeds of love, with gentle hand plow. Carefully tend, and watch your garden grow." ~ RBG

HOLIDAY INSIGHTS

And Truths Learned From The Path

New Years

Easter

Mother's Day

Father's Day

Thanksgiving

Christmas

"A Little Dab A Do Ya!"

HAPPY NEW YEAR!

Got resolutions? Broke any yet?

I have watched so many over the holidays trying to *cram in* all they did not get done by the end of the year. One thing I noticed was people trying to make time for God. People were running around stores looking for *symbols* of their faith to show others they *got Christ*. Unfortunately, many get by with *a little dab a do ya*. I know I have dated myself because most of you reading that phrase have no idea what product had that slogan. Look it up and you will understand. Many Christians treat God that way, *a little dab a do ya*.

Wearing a cross, a fish on the car or going to a service once a week; this is how many treat God. Daily reading of His word or praying more than at mealtimes are replaced with, "Will you fix this Lord?" prayers. At the end of the year, with all the Christmas traditions, once-a week Christians get a guilt complex. Sadly where ever you look you see that children and adults are wrapped up in the holidays as portrayed by the world and not as portrayed by His word.

Why is it every December all the Christians are wearing buttons that say, "Keep Christ in Christmas" or "Jesus is the Reason"? Only in December are their cars and homes depicting the Nativity and other Christian symbols. What about the other eleven months? What are we Christians saying? Sadly, "a little God will do us."

NEW YEAR'S RESOLUTION: Keeping Christ in every day. You cannot do this in your own strength. You will need His strength. So, rise early to read His word and pray. You make time for other things in your day. Can you find more than "a little dab" of time for Him? Unlike other religions, our faith allows us to pray unceasingly, anytime and anywhere. It is a symptom of our heart's condition; walking with Him by our side talking anytime, anywhere, and anyhow. Make your relationship with Him by faith, not simply a religious practice. Then, the other eleven months of the year, people are seeing you keep Christ in the whole year by how you keep Him in your life daily.

By God's grace and strength this year I will:

[1] Therefore, brothers, by the mercies of God, I urge you to present your bodies as a living sacrifice, holy and pleasing to God; this is your spiritual worship. [2] Do not be conformed to this age, but be transformed by the renewing of your mind, so that you may discern what is the good, pleasing, and perfect will of God. [3] For by the grace given to me, I tell everyone among you not to think of himself more highly than he should think. Instead, think sensibly, as God has distributed a measure of faith to each one. [4] Now as we have many parts in one body, and all the parts do not have the same function, [5] in the same way we who are many are one body in Christ and individually members of one another. [6] According to the grace given to us, we have different gifts: If prophecy, use it according to the standard of one's faith; [7] if service, in service; if teaching, in teaching; [8] if exhorting, in exhortation; giving, with generosity; leading, with diligence; showing mercy, with cheerfulness. [9] Love must be without hypocrisy. Detest evil; cling to what is good. [10] Show family affection to one another with brotherly love. Outdo one another in showing honor. [11] Do not lack diligence; be fervent in spirit; serve the Lord. [12] Rejoice in hope; be patient in affliction; be persistent in prayer. [13] Share with the saints in their needs;

pursue hospitality. [14] Bless those who persecute you; bless and do not curse. [15] Rejoice with those who rejoice; weep with those who weep. [16] Agree with one another. Do not be proud; instead, associate with the humble. Do not be wise in your own estimation. [17] Do not repay anyone evil for evil. Try to do what is honorable in everyone's eyes. [18] If possible, on your part, live at peace with everyone. [19] Friends do not avenge yourselves; instead, leave room for His wrath. For it is written: Vengeance belongs to Me; I will repay, says the Lord. [20]But, if your enemy is hungry, feed him. If he is thirsty, give him something to drink. For in so doing you will be heaping fiery coals on his head. [21] Do not be conquered by evil but conquer evil with good. *(Romans 12 HCSB)*

You may be the only Christ some people see; the only Bible they will ever read.

Happy New Year!

May You Feel Jesus Near, Every Day Of This Year!

EMPTY TOMB EASTERCOOKIES

The day before Easter prepare and make these cookies as a family remembrance and lesson.

You will need:

- Bible
- Ziplock baggie
- 1 c. Whole pecans
- A wooden spoon or rubber kitchen mallet
- 1 teaspoon. Vinegar
- 3 Egg whites
- Pinch of salt
- 1 c. Sugar
- Tape (kind that will not leave adhesive behind when removed like painters tape.)

Preheat your oven to 300 degrees.

- **Action**: Seal pecans in Ziplock bag. Have children beat them with spoon/mallet breaking them into small pieces.
- **Story**: Jesus was arrested and beaten by Roman soldiers.
- **Scripture**: *John 19:1-3.*

Add the 1 teaspoon. vinegar to mixing bowl

- **Action**: Allow children to smell the vinegar; place their fingertip on a drop and let them taste if they will.

- **Story**: Jesus was thirsty on the cross and they gave Him vinegar to drink.
- **Scripture**: *John 19:28-30*

Add egg whites into vinegar

- **Action**: Add egg whites to bowl.
- **Story**: Egg whites represent Jesus' life He gave up giving us life.
- **Scripture**: *John 10:10-11.*

Add a pinch of salt in mixing bowl

- **Action**: Sprinkle some grains of salt into each participant's hand. Ask them to taste the salt.
- **Story**: The salt is a symbol of the salty tears shed by Jesus' followers at the Cross. And it tastes of the bitterness of our own sin to Jesus that He willingly carried to the Cross.
- **Scripture**: Luke 23:27.

Story: Ask the family if they think what is in the bowl tastes good.

Add 1 cup of sugar

- **Action:** Dip a spoon in bowl and let them taste if they want.
- **Story**: Jesus died on the Cross because He loves us. That is the sweetness of Salvation, His free gift. He died because He wants us to know, love and belong to Him.
- **Scripture**: Psalm 34:8 and John 3:16.

Beat egg whites on high speed ten or more minutes until stiff peaks form.

- **Story**: The white color of the cookies represents purity. In God's eyes, all that accept His death, burial and resurrection are cleansed and their sins are forgiven. They are pure and white as snow.
- **Scripture**: *Isaiah 1:18, and John 3:1-3.*

Fold in broken nut pieces. Drop teaspoon size mounds onto a cookie sheet lined with waxed paper.

- **Story**: Each of these mounds is a symbol of Jesus' rocky tomb where He was placed after He was taken down off the Cross.
- **Scripture**: Matthew 27:57-60.

Place cookie sheet in oven door and turn oven off.

- **Action**: Place a piece of tape as a SEAL to the oven door.
- **Story**: They sealed Jesus' tomb.
- **Scripture**: Matthew 28:65-66.
- **Story**: It is bedtime. It is safe to leave the oven sealed overnight. The followers of Jesus were scared and sad. They probably did not sleep well that night once the tomb was sealed. But we know we can.
- **Scripture:** John 16:20 and 22.

Sunrise Easter Morning**:**

- **Action**: Easter morning, open the oven and leave the door open. When the family comes in remove the sheet and let them each take a cookie.
- **Story**: The surface is cracked. The tomb was open, Jesus was not there. When they bite into the cookies, they will find them hollow, empty.

The First Easter

- **Scripture**: Matthew 28:1-9.

He is Risen, He is Risen Indeed!

ANCHOR, MOM

Dateline Mother's Day: Every Mother's Day I find myself defending the word Mom and what a mom really is in the world. No adjectives needed. Mom says it all.

My daughters were home visiting. My oldest was here from overseas with my two darling granddaughters. My youngest was here from Montana, expecting her first child December 18th. I had been busy being mom. I commented about *always being a mom* to Susan, a pastor's wife, who gave me the title for this blog: *Anchor, Mom.* I do not know if she coined it, but I am borrowing the phrase.

An *Anchor, Mom* may be a mom, grandmother, aunt, favorite cousin, even a school teacher, Sunday School teacher; maybe even a neighbor. They are the women God places in every child's life to nurture and guide them in Him. They are an *anchor, a mom.*

I *hate* all the adjectives people add to the word Mom these days and have various appropriate answers. Every time I hear an adjective added to the name Mom I just want to cringe. Quit apologizing. Mom says it all and is all sufficient, no apology needed. You are more than an added adjective to the name Mom.

When others describe you; how you should answer?

1. Stay at home mom? No, I am let out of the house as needed.
2. Work outside of your home? Yes, I work at school and church events; athletics and club events. I am the shopper for groceries

and home supplies. I am banker, the Mom taxi, and numerous other positions.

3. Are you a fulltime mom? Should there be any other kind?
4. Are you a domestic Engineer? Do not even get me started on this one
5. Are you a homemaker? No, my builder built my home.

You are getting the idea. I finally close such discussions with, "is there anything wrong with just saying Mom? Does not the word Mom say it all? Mary was *just* a mom to Jesus. When talking with mom's I would say, "as well as being a mom what else do you manage?" This is where you can talk about the additional career job, the care of elderly parents, etc.

Moms are always explaining themselves almost as in excuse of not being something more. Why? The world devalues moms. The name Mom should say it all. However, I am adding *Anchor*, Mom today. Not as an adjective, but more of a station. These are the women that are always *Moms*, even if they have no children of their own. These are the anchors of stability, *Moms* who have been promoted to Grandmoms or, are aunts, teachers, and the neighbors, which see a need and heed God's prompting and intervene in a child's life.

God thinks a lot about Moms and places great value on mothers and women in His word. He places them as anchors. Even in death Jesus looked down from the cross and thought of His own mother's needs.

> When Jesus saw his mother and the disciple whom he loved standing nearby, he said to his mother, "Woman, behold, your son!"(John 19:26)

> Naomi was a mother-in-law to Ruth that acted as a true MOM when she realized that Ruth still needed her. *(Ruth 1:18)*.

You never stop being a mom, you just spread out your wings and gather more under your wings. The world has devalued motherhood making moms feel worthless. Some women fear motherhood and the loss of personal freedom and value. Being a mom is not for wimps, cowards, or the selfish, it is for those whom God chooses. If you are lucky enough to be chosen as a *mom*, remember God uses His weakest vessels, like Mary, to accomplish His greatest works and He supplies all you will need. For Christian women it should be the greatest honor to be a birth Mom and/ or an Anchor, Mom. Do not get caught up in the world's opinion.

God places great value on you as a woman. The Bible mentions weddings, names the girl and who her father was, thereby giving her heritage and establishing the lineage of Christ. These women linked Mary to the house of David. They were not *no-name* unimportant females. There was Deborah who was a prophetess and a judge. (Judges 4:4), Queen Esther whom God used to deliver His people and of course Mary, the mother of Jesus. God did not need to bring Jesus into the world using a woman. He could have just had Jesus appear with no mention of how He arrived. There are many significant women that were important women in the Bible as well as moms.

Where ever God places you currently is important to Him so do not bemoan your lot in life. God has a plan and a purpose that changes with age. You were born for such a time; to be a mother. Embrace your roll. I had raised my girls who are now moms themselves. They still need their mom on occasion. My husband still needed me. Yet God placed me in full time work at a Christian bookstore. He laid it on my heart to write my blog and children books, parenting book and church youth musicals. I still had a full plate. I was just filling it from a different buffet line.

Accept what God has for you to do today. Do not begrudge, belittle, or let satan* lie to you about your worth. Seek God's will and enjoy the journey.

*satan – Always the snake, so satan, devil, etc. still in lower case, as he always is one.

FATHER'S DAY

Consequences

Your actions equal reactions. For every cause there is an effect. For some reason too many people do not see that their actions affect anyone other than themselves. Consider the angry driver that speeds out of sight as the two cars they swerved through head for ditches; the over-eating, over-drinking or over-smoking family member that says it only hurts them; or the teenage who swears it is their life to mess up and none of your business. As you are reading those scenarios you can easily find the consequences. Yet, every day we act without seeing the long-range effect on our actions. The *lecture* on consequences is one of my most discussed with students.

Children often need to be reminded that their actions have consequences, good ones and bad ones. If we really look at examples of both, we easily see it is good actions that everyone benefits the most from. Visuals often make things more understandable. It may seem simplistic but, take a bucket of water, a tub, pool or lake and toss something in the water. Have you ever tried to toss something in so that the water is not disturbed? It is impossible. No matter what you try to do, you will not be able to pass the object through the water without disturbing the surface; the bigger the item, the bigger the reaction, or consequence.

Choices, we make them every day and our actions always have reactions or consequences. What defines our actions? What affects our choices?

What we read, hear, see = our thoughts

1.   What we think = attitude
2.   Our attitude = character
3.   Our character = actions

If someone's actions are negative they cause negative reactions which means they must change what they read, hear and see. It is important to show the flip side of the coin by praising positive actions that equaled positive reactions. For example, studying, doing homework, etc. equals better grades. Or, showing respect and consideration equals receiving respect and consideration, which results in more privileges and responsibility.

Unfortunately, we are in a world ruled by sin. Sin is a huge pebble thrown in the pond and its' ripples are the consequences that are far-reaching, even into the next generations. In 1 Samuel 3 the Bible tells of Eli's penalty for not stopping his sons' actions. Eli paid the price of *inaction* over his sons' *actions*.

> 11And the Lord said to Samuel: "See, I am about to do something in Israel that will make the ears of everyone who hears of it tingle. 12At that time I will carry out against Eli everything I spoke against his family—from beginning to end. 13For I told him that I would judge his family forever because of the sin he knew about; his sons made themselves contemptible, and he failed to restrain them. 14Therefore, I swore to the house of Eli, 'The guilt of Eli's house will never be atoned for by sacrifice or offering.

Eli's sin was allowing desecration of the house of the Lord. He knew about what his sons were doing and did nothing. Eli, as a father, knew what his children were up to and did absolutely nothing.

I know parents who have thrown in the towel over their minor children and said, "What can I do?" Everything you can do is what God expects. God holds mothers and fathers responsible for how their children act, what they read, hear and see if they are under their roof. The problem is, parents allow things to slip by until the children are so out of control it will take a war to win. Some say they pick their battles, but that usually means they finally exit the war. Raising children is spiritual warfare and the other side is not sitting idle.

Inaction *is* an action. When I heard two boys in the classroom discussing hitting back over a senseless killing, I could have kept walking out of the class room and ignored them. Trust me, it is easier. However, I knew they saw I heard them. I had that *feeling* you get inside when you know you are supposed to speak and it was choking me to get out. So I went back and looked at the young man and asked, "What will that do?" He said, "I will get even, I can't just do nothing." I looked at him and said, "You cannot throw a rock in the water and not expect a splash." Blunt statements that seem senseless usually get attention (action/reaction). I then asked him, "What if they get even and hit you back?" He said, "We all got to die sometime." Death is not a feared consequence any more, it is a badge to wear. We have desensitized a whole generation. I asked him if he thought someone would get even for him and he said he thought they would. I then asked him, "What if it is your grandmother, or your mother, or baby sister they hit next and how will those left behind feel then?" I had his attention. First, death is not the end of anything, even if you do not believe in afterlife. Second, there are those left behind after a shooting, suicide, death or self-inflicted cancer. Even if you die, someone is forced to live with your action's consequences. People recognize you by your actions.

> 16 By their fruit you will recognize them. Do people pick grapes from thorn bushes, or figs from thistles? 17 Likewise every good tree bears good fruit, but a bad tree bears bad fruit. 18 A good tree cannot bear bad fruit, and a bad tree cannot bear good fruit. 19 Every tree that does not bear good fruit is cut down and thrown into the fire. 20 Thus, by their fruit you will recognize them. *(Matthew 7:16-20)*

Your actions define what kind of tree you are. Regardless if you are a father, mother, or child, your actions ripple through other's lives. What will your actions cause today?

TRUTH OR TRADITION?

Traditions are great. They help us remember and pass on family, heritage, and faith to next generations. Until they do not. When traditions morph into legends that take over to the point that the original point is obscure, then it is time to rethink, reevaluate and reform. I believe that some Christmas traditions need to be evaluated.

Growing up mom said, as did many preachers and older Christians:

> "If it does not ring true, if you are not sure … if it sounds different from what you have heard, go to The Word, His Word. What does The Bible say?"

I challenge you to check it out. Check me out. Do not blindly accept what you hear or read. Always compare to God's Word.

Over the holidays I finally caught *The Three Kings* celebration performance at a local public presentation. I also viewed many manger scenes. Many churches put on a *Walk Through Bethlehem* or, a Christmas pageant. While many were impressive, I was stunned at what was presented as fact. The Bible is readily available in most people groups' native tongue, so it is easily found what God's Word give as an account for Jesus' birth. The shepherds and the wise men are spoke of and their actions described. The Gospels give facts and facts matter. No words are there by accident. They are there for a reason.

Luke 2

Joseph and Mary *were not* immigrants. Joseph was returning to his homeland for a government required census. Shame on churches that used Jesus' birth as a political statement. Some presented them in separate, caged stalls; as detained illegal immigrants. Joseph was obeying man's law for God's sake. *(Romans 13)* He was not an immigrant, and he certainly was not detained against his will. Nor was he separated from Mary and Jesus. Jesus' birth used as a political statement by a church is horrible. There was no tradition or legend to blame here. It was simply changing facts to suit an agenda. You do not change a character, a story line or setting to suit an agenda, regardless the author. Shame on those churches. Not hard to figure which church type in Revelations they represented.

> Joseph also went up from Galilee, from the city of Nazareth, to Judea, to the city of David which is called Bethlehem, because he was of the house and family of David, in order to register along with Mary, who was engaged to him, and was with child.*(Luke 2:4-5 NASB)*

He was placed in a manger. The manger was the feeding trough. There was no hay. There were no animals. It was most likely of a harden clay/brick form. The shepherds were in the field with the flocks. The manger was empty. The stable was empty. That is why they could use it.

> And while they were there, the time came for her to give birth. And she gave birth to her firstborn son and wrapped him in swaddling cloths and laid him in a manger, because there was no place for them in the inn. *(Luke 2:6-7 ESV)*

According to Jewish historical facts the temple had shepherds for the sacrificial animals. It was springtime in Bethlehem. (Not December, but that is okay.) That is why they were in the field at night. It was warm enough. These shepherds may have been guarding the temple flock from which the sacrifices came. Temple shepherds would know what an unblemished lamb wrapped in a manger meant.

Unto you is born this day in the city of David a Savior, who is Christ the Lord. And this will be a sign for you: you will find a baby wrapped in swaddling cloths and lying in a manger. *(Luke 2:11- 12)*

When a sacrifice required an unblemished lamb, the newborn lamb was wrapped in swaddling cloth so it could not be marred or bruised. Then it was placed in the unused stable's manger awaiting sacrifice; protected from bruising or marring. It was a sacrificial lamb. Jesus was the unblemished, sacrificial lamb. That is why He was wrapped in swaddling clothes and placed in the manger. He was the last sacrifice ever to be needed.

Yes, the song says the cattle were there. They were not. Again, that is okay. This traditional idea does not deter from the meaning of Jesus' birth.

Give a visual of Jesus birth. Spread out your nativity figures throughout the room. Make a field for shepherds and animals. Place the magi on the East side of the room. If Jesus is separate from your manger, place him in manger on Christmas morn. Wrap Him in a bit of cloth. Be detailed in teaching children and grandchildren as well as visitors. It is a great conversation start up.

There are other unfortunate traditions but, I will end with the Magi ones. Three kings at the stable. no the scriptures say Magi. Nowhere in the Bible does it say kings or that there were only three. May be there were a dozen traveling together. Some beliefs state there were a dozen. That they were kings is a tradition that seems to be linked by some to Isaiah 60 and Psalm 72 referring to kings bearing gifts. It really does not matter. It is like the three crosses on Calvary Hill. Only three crosses are shown at Easter because Jesus had a man on either side that spoke to each other. There were many more crucified that day as there were on most days.

There were three gifts so there must have only been three kings is the assumption. We take tradition as fact. It simple is not in the bible. Nowhere does it say three kings and certainly they are not named in the Bible. Somewhere along the 6th century a historian decided there were three and what their names were.

Tradition was born. The names came out of traditional Persian history. It was supposed they were Gaspar, Balthasar, and Melchior. Magi were wise men. It is in the plural form so more than one. Wise men were scholars of law and historians; advisors to kings.

Three gifts meant three kings to some and it soon became fact, tradition, and finally legend. They brought three gifts, gold, frankincense, and myrrh. Again, three gifts specified for specific reasons. That should be the emphasis. The gifts had a spiritual significance as well. Gold was offered to kings on earth and frankincense was offered to deities. Myrrh was an embalming substance and symbolized death. They were extremely specific references to Jesus' birth, death, and resurrection. The gifts were brought to the house where Jesus lived. Jesus was not a baby but, was still under two years old.

So, here are the facts. Magi were never present at the stable and neither should yours be in your nativity scene. I always place mine on the other side of the room, as though traveling from afar; on the East side of the room.

According to historical references, wise men, educators, and philosophers in the east studied history from other areas, including Hebrew scrolls. They knew of prophecies and references to the star, to the Messiah. So, when the star appeared, they went searching.

> After Jesus was born in Bethlehem of Judea in the days of King Herod, wise men from the east arrived unexpectedly in Jerusalem, [2] saying, "Where is He who has been born King of the Jews? For we saw His star in the east and have come to worship Him." [3] When King Herod heard this, he was deeply disturbed, and all Jerusalem with him. [4] So he assembled all the chief priests and scribes of the people and asked them where the Messiah would be born. [5] "In Bethlehem of Judea," they told him, "because this is what was written by the prophet: [6] and you, Bethlehem, in the land of Judah, are by no means least among the leaders of Judah: because out of you will come a leader who will shepherd My people Israel. "[7] Then Herod secretly

summoned the wise men and asked them the exact time the star appeared. He sent them to Bethlehem and said, "Go and search carefully for the child. When you find Him, report back to me so that I too can go and worship Him. "[9] After hearing the king, they went on their way. And there it was—the star they had seen in the east! It led them until it came and stopped above the place where the child was. [10] When they saw the star, they were overjoyed beyond measure. [11] Entering the house, they saw the child with Mary His mother, and falling to their knees, they worshiped Him. Then they opened their treasures and presented Him with gifts: gold, frankincense, and myrrh. [16] Then Herod, when he saw that he had been outwitted by the wise men, flew into a rage. He gave orders to massacre all the male children in and around Bethlehem who were two years old and under, in keeping with the time he had learned from the wise men. *(Luke 2:4-5 NASB)*

Herod killed children up to two years of age based on when they had seen the star. The star was over Jesus birth place. Jesus was no longer in the stable, not a baby. The wise men entered a house. In 2020 people became all excited about a *star* they labeled *Christmas Star* for its unusual appearance at Christmas and only showing up every few hundred years. The real Christmas Star was followed for two years and was set in place by God's hand. It was not an occurrence for a night every few hundred years at Christmas time. People cheapen the Word of God by adding to it to make them *feel* something. Christianity is not a *feel good* faith. Walking close with the Lord is a heart knowledge, not an emotional one.

Much of what is wrong with the world's views of Christians is because of the discrepancies that traditions have brought into the various portions of the Bible through the years. It is never too late to set the record straight. It is never unimportant to stick to the facts. It might be difficult, but I think it is important we go back to His Word and tell the story of Christmas as it was written with all the significant details and emphasis. There is nothing in God's Word by accident or in a random order, ever.

REFERENCES

Tucker, Tanya *"Strong Enough To Bend"*. Tanya Tucker Capital, 1988 Album

Head, Mark. "Solid Rock." *Mark Head*. Green Albums, 1975. Album

Believe. (n.d.) In Merriam-Webster's online dictionary [*believe*] (11th ed.) Retrieved from http://www.merriam-webster.com/dictionary/mania

Apologetics (n.d.) In Merriam-Webster's online dictionary [apologetics] (11th ed.) Retrieved from http://www.merriam-webster.com/dictionary/mania

believe https://en.wikipedia.org/wiki/Believelieve in

apologetics https://en.wikipedia.org/wiki/Apologetics

Printed in the United States
by Baker & Taylor Publisher Services